No Safe Harbor
Essays About Pirate Politics

United States Pirate Party

ISBN: 1468033999
ISBN-13: 978-1468033991

The only way to deal with an unfree world is to become so absolutely free that your very existence is an act of rebellion. - Albert Camus

Where this age differs from those immediately preceding it is that a liberal intelligentsia is lacking. Bully-worship, under various disguises, has become a universal religion, and such truisms as that a machine-gun is still a machine-gun even when a "good" man is squeezing the trigger have turned into heresies which it is actually becoming dangerous to utter. – George Orwell

Timid men prefer the calm of despotism to the tempestuous sea of liberty. – Thomas Jefferson

To deprive a man of his natural liberty and to deny to him the ordinary amenities of life is worse then starving the body; it is starvation of the soul, the dweller in the body. – Mohandas Gandhi

DEDICATION

This book is dedicated to all of those who would educate themselves about the political issues of our time and seek to change the course of events by becoming embroiled in that change.

CONTENTS

Foreword   1

Government and Corporate Transparency and Accountability

Assassinating Citizens   4
    Marcus Kesler
The Worst Part of Citizenship   9
    Ryan Moffitt
The Parable of the Pasture   13
    Howard Denson
Indie Authors Shaking the Pillars of Publishing   19
    Reagen Dandridge Desilets

Breaking the Two Party Two-Step   25
    Andrew "K'Tetch" Norton
Fluid Democracy   31
    William Sims Bainbridge
Privatizing Life   63
    Kembrew McLeod
Killing the Corporate Person   84
    Andrew "K'tetch" Norton

Privacy

"Real Names" Policies Are An Abuse of Power   90
    danah boyd
Criminal of Innocence   96
    Travis McCrea
Privacy Now, Nothing Later   102
    Ryan Moffitt
Personal Privacy   105
    Travis McCrea
Notes on the 4th Amendment   108
    The Electronic Frontier Foundation
No Safe Quarter   130
    Loreley MacTavish
The Universal Declaration of Human Rights   135
    The United Nations

CONTENTS CONTINUED

Intellectual Property

History of Copyright   146
Rick Falkvinge

The DRM Sausage Factory   168
Cory Doctorow

Pirates   179
Lawrence Lessig

Questions Concerning Copyright   188
Brad Hall

This Gene is Your Gene   202
Kembrew McLeod

About the Authors   213

Further Reading   219

References   222

Get Involved   235

Mimi and Eunice comics throughout by Nina Paley on pages 3, 24, 83, 89, 101, 104, 134, 144, 145, 178, and 212.

ACKNOWLEDGMENTS

The United States Pirate Party would like to thank all of those who allowed us to use their material, either that which existed before we edited this book, or those who saw a hole that needed filling and helped fill it. We salute you.

We would also like to thank you, the reader. Just as a tree that falls in a forest may not make a sound if there is no one around to hear it, so too it goes with words. Words, with no one around to read them, never change worlds.

FOREWORD

The first Pirate Party was founded on January 1, 2006 by Rick Falkvinge in Sweden.

Six months later, similar parties started to spring up all over the world. All of these parties started off with the same singular goal of intellectual property reform. But, these disparate parties realized that the roots of the world's problems ran deeper than even intellectual property reform could fix.

With time, these parties added many more items to their platform. These can be condensed into 3 topics - Government and Corporate Transparency and Accountability, Personal Privacy, and, of course, Intellectual Property reform.

If nothing else, 2011 will be seen as the year of the uprisings. The year began with the Arab Spring, in which the citizens of various Middle Eastern countries rose up and either overthrew their governments or caused massive changes in their governing structures. Later in the year - September - the Occupy Wall Street movement began and quickly spread across the United States and to every continent except Antarctica.

Who knows what 2012 will bring.

No Safe Harbor

The problem the Pirate Party faces, and clearly, every third party, is "Who are they? What do they stand for? Why should I vote for them?"

This book seeks to help alleviate that problem. To that end we have written a series of essays related to our primary platform. We decided to do this for several reasons. These reasons also mirror our platform.

The main reason is transparency. If we allow our platform to be plainly visible to anyone who wants to know it, then we have an even greater reason to follow it to the letter.

The second reason is personal privacy. We do not ask that you tell us who you are or where you are or any other personal information when you download this book from any of the USPP websites (if you downloaded it from there).

The third reason, mirrors the intellectual property reform we seek. We have licensed this book under a Creative Commons license. You can do anything you want to with this book. Email it to anyone, copy passages, post pieces to your website, whatever. As long as your use is not commercial, it should be allowed.

The fourth is that of education. An ignorant man looks in the mirror, likes what he sees and is happy with that. The wise man looks in the mirror, sees what he does not know, and is always questioning that which he does know. So we are left with a hope that many will read this who do NOT agree with us, but are willing to open their minds to other possibilities. That it will lead to self-investigation of topics, and a broader, better informed conversation on the topic. Only when we have dialogues of substance, free of spirited invective, fear mongering, soundbites, and claims fabricated from whole cloth, can we start addressing the problems properly.

The United States Pirate Party December 1, 2011

Government and Corporate Transparency and Accountability

ASSASSINATING CITIZENS
MARCUS KESLER

On September 30th, 2011, the CIA targeted and killed a citizen of the United States overseas. The citizen was Anwar Al-Awlaki, a Yemen-American born in New Mexico who was living in Yemen where he practiced his religion as an Imam and who has been accused of hiding in Yemen to avoid capture for his suspected roles in various terrorist attacks against the United States.

In December of last year, Al-Awlaki's father filed suit against the Justice Department to stop the targeted killing of his son as authorized by President Obama. US District Judge John Bates dismissed the case, stating that his father had no standing to file suit and that a judicial consideration regarding the extrajudicial execution of a US citizen would have to wait another day [1]. Lawyers for the US Government would not confirm that Al-Awlaki was targeted for execution, but stated that Al-Awlaki could always file suit himself or present himself to US authorities.

The argument made by the Justice Department was that a US citizen has to file suit and present himself to a court in order to prove that the Government has no authorization to execute him, that he is guilty until he proves himself innocent. This decision appears to stand in stark contrast to the 5th

Amendment of the Constitution of the United States, which would seem to offer multiple protections to a US citizen in this case:

1. The right to have a grand jury hear the case that the Justice Department brings against them, to decide if there is enough evidence to proceed with a trial. Crimes punishable by death must be tried after indictment. The Government never made its case in a court of law, instead it argued before Judge Bates that the burden of proof that Al-Awlaki should not be executed lies with him. This also appears to bring forth another aspect of the 5th Amendment, self incrimination.

2. The 5th Amendment states that a witness may not be forced to testify if such testimony could lead to the witness incriminating himself. Requiring a person to argue why they should not be executed without due process, instead of filing a case against such a person and arguing to a jury why this person should be executed, would certainly result in self incrimination. Another important distinction to make is that asserting your right to remain silent and refusing to testify does not imply guilt. The Supreme Court reinforced in 2001 that this constitutional safeguard exists specifically for the innocent, stating in their ruling of Ohio v. Reiner that "This Court has never held, however, that the privilege is unavailable to those who claim innocence. To the contrary, the Court has emphasized that one of the Fifth Amendment's basic functions is to protect innocent persons who might otherwise be ensnared by ambiguous circumstances." [2] The common assumption of "If he won't testify against himself, then he must have something to hide" is simply not supported in judicial case law, and the framers intention was clearly to protect US citizens from an aggressive Government.

3. Due Process: A person may not be deprived of life, liberty, or property without "due process." The Government is held to abide by the law of the land, even if the person stands accused of violating the law. The argument of "the person is accused of breaking the law of the land, so he lost the protection of the same laws" does not stand.

No Safe Harbor

Since the beginning of this "War on Terror" the role of constitutional safeguards when dealing with accused terrorists has been a question that has been raised multiple times. When these questions are raised inside a court of law, the preferred tactic of the Justice Department has been to raise the issue of "national security." The argument is they cannot answer questions, because answering them would place the United States in danger. So not only is the burden of proof on the accused, but the Government argues that it does not have to defend itself because doing so would harm national security. When the Government does give an answer, usually outside a court of law to avoid establishing case law that could hinder its operations in the future, the answers include various arguments about how constitutional safeguards do not apply to individual cases:

1. When news surfaced about the actions of US soldiers in Abu Ghraib, people started to question if these actions violated our laws or international laws. The argument was that since the prisoners were neither US citizens, nor held on US soil, no constitutional safeguards applied. The remaining question on whether these actions violated international law was never fully answered either.

2. When presented with news regarding the detainment and torture/enhanced interrogation of enemy combatants at the Guantanamo Bay Detention Camp located inside the Guantanamo Bay Naval Base the question of constitutional safeguards was raised again. This time the Government was acting inside US jurisdiction, located on land under the control of the United States Government leased from Cuba. The argument was raised that since the land was controlled by the Government, the law of the land applies and must be followed by the Government. The Justice Department argued that since the detainees were not US citizens and classified as enemy combatants, no constitutional rights exist that would protect the detainees. The mantra repeated by supporters of these actions was "if you are not American, you are not protected by the Constitution."

3. Anwar Al-Awlaki was a United States citizen, and as such should have been protected by Constitutional safeguards. The main argument against giving enemy combatants the protections guaranteed by our Constitution has been the lack of citizenship. "American Rights are only for Americans" could not be used as a disqualification for Al-Awlaki. Instead the Justice Department issued a memo with the opinion that war is due process enough [3]. Instead of trying him before a court to decide if he has committed a crime worthy of the death penalty, which would be the definition of due process, it was decided that the fact that we are at war and think he is on the wrong side was enough due process to justify an extrajudicial execution (otherwise known as an assassination).

So we now have a very slippery slope. When the "War on Terror" started, the enemy was "them" and they had no rights. Then the enemy became "foreigners on foreign soil" and they had no rights. Once we were acclimated to that assumption, the enemy became "foreigners on US soil" and they had no rights. Now the enemy can be a US citizen, who has no rights, and can be assassinated at the discretion of the executive branch of our Government. Who will be the next person or group to be summarily stripped of the protections granted to them by our Constitution?

After the Oklahoma City Bombing, a terrorist attack orchestrated and executed by an American citizen, Timothy McVeigh was not assassinated. He was arrested, indicted, tried in a court of law, and then executed. Following the Fort Hood shooting, Nidal Malik Hasan is awaiting court martial for his accused crimes. After the Tuscon Shooting, Jared Lee Loughner was arrested and has been indicted for the attempted assassination of a member of the House of Representatives. He is awaiting trial, and is still considered innocent until he has been found guilty by a court of law. Here we have three American citizens who have been accused of terrorism and murder, who are given full due process as guaranteed to them by the Constitution of the United States. Anwar Al-Awlaki was accused of committing many crimes against fellow citizens of the United States, but he has never been charged with the act of taking another persons life. The accusations against him include hateful speech, inciting violence, calling for the murder of fellow Americans, even training others how to kill Americans. And for these accusations he was executed by the CIA. It appears that if you are accused of killing your fellow citizens, you are entitled to due process in accordance with our Constitution. But if you are accused of training or encouraging others to kill your fellow citizens, you can be assassinated without any judicial proceeding at all.

Where will this development lead us? Should our Government be able to declare that US citizens who speak out against the Constitution lose all constitutional protections? What makes a citizen an enemy combatant? It appears that rhetoric may be enough, since even citizens who stand accused of murder are entitled to due process. Does speaking out against the United States and its Government meet the threshold of abandoning your own constitutional safeguards?

If so, then what will stop our Government from deciding that protesters in the United States who speak out against their country have surrendered their constitutional rights? What about members of the Tea Party movement who are fighting against their government and speak about "watering the tree of liberty with the blood of tyrants"? The current actions of our Government is reminiscent of the Cold War, but the majority of people would have expected these actions from the "other guys."

We believed in truth, justice, and the American way; and assassination of its own citizens was something the "communists" would do. The United States has entered a dangerous time in our history and we must decide which path we want to take. Do we want to remain on the path where the Constitution is absolute, our rights are inalienable, and justice prevails? Or do we follow the darker path, where justice is achieved without a judge, rights are ignored, and the Constitution cast aside when convenient. And if we follow that path, who will be the next group that gets edited out of our Constitution?

THE WORST PART OF CENSORSHIP IS [THIS PHRASE HAS BEEN SEIZED BY ICE]
RYAN MOFFITT

Anyone who has been within 100 yards of a television, radio or computer in the last 30 years or so has heard of .com, .net, .org, et cetera. These are top level domains (TLDs) and serve as the first step in pointing your web browser in the direction you want it to go. TLDs are hosted on root domain servers around the world, and serve as the backbone for the internet as we know it today. In a perfect world, these servers would hum along, receiving periodic maintenance and let us surf on our merry little way.

But by this point, you've probably learned that we don't live in a perfect world.

These TLDs have come under attack, and it's not from your usual e-terrorist wielding a zombie botnet army. The U.S Department of Homeland Security has been on the attack, wielding the Immigration and Customs Enforcement Agency (ICE), a $5 billion annual budget and hundreds of special agents trained in intimidation tactics and the latest in technological expertise. The ICE Cyber Crimes Unit has undertaken operations to forcibly remove websites from the .com, .net and .org TLDs for supposed intellectual property violations. Dubbed

"Operation Within Our Sites," ICE never informed the rightful owners of the sites they were being investigated, and the operators of the sites did not find out about the seizure until they discovered it themselves. When they contacted their webspace provider, they were simply given the name and number of an ICE Special Agent, who refused to comment on ongoing investigations. As of the publishing date of this book, Within Our Sites has seized at least 90 known websites and has severely interrupted service for 82,000 others in various technical foul-ups and miscommunications.

Now this all sounds fairly terrible, doesn't it? Big Brother stepping over free speech and all that again, right? Well, here's where it gets a bit more complicated.

Remember those root name servers? Those servers aren't always operated by altruistic organizations who have your best interest in mind. I'll use .com and .net as an example, as the overwhelming majority of websites you navigate to will be in the .com and .net TLD. The root name servers for these two domains are owned and operated by a private corporation called Verisign. As the operator of the largest root name servers in the world, the Department of Homeland Security, the Department of Justice and ICE have put the figurative screws to Verisign. When asked about this development, the US government argues that because Verisign is an American company, it has the unrestricted and unilateral power to shut down entire portions of the .com and .net domains, whether or not the sites are hosted on American servers or owned by American citizens. Through ICE pressure, censorship-friendly judges issued sealed court orders to Verisign, who promptly took down the supposedly infringing sites without so much as a question asked.

It gets worse still.

Verisign, fearing further pressure from not only ICE, but from local and federal law enforcement agencies, and seeking to dodge criticism for taking down domains that had been ruled legal in other localities, filed an astonishing and unprecedented request with the Internet Corporation for Assigned Names and Numbers (ICANN), the organization in charge of assigning IP addresses and managing all of the TLDs in October 2011. This request was for ICANN to allow Verisign to shut off websites in the .com and .net TLDs when simply asked by a law enforcement agency, without requiring so much as a court order, search and seizure warrant or even a phone call from a judge. This power would apply to any website, hosted and/or owned by anyone, anywhere in the world and without any form of due process. The proposed rules, to the surprise of nobody, were crafted with the assistance of US Immigration and Customs Enforcement, the Departments of Justice and Homeland Security and the Federal Bureau of Investigation and proposed by what has now become the puppet organization Verisign.

The justification presented to us by these organizations for warrantless property seizure, in clear violation of the 4th Amendment has been to "control intellectual property infringement in the digital age."

That's right, folks. Your constitutional rights are inconvenient to Hollywood. A free society is not conducive to shoving chunks of human culture in a box and setting armed guards in front of it. Hollywood's heavy-weights believe so heavily in censoring the internet, they held a little meeting in May, 2007. The US Chamber of Commerce (a corporate lobbying organization not to be confused with the US Department of Commerce) held a seminar in Stockholm entitled "Sweden – A Safe Haven for Pirates?" The speaker, Johan Schluter of the IP lobbyist group, Danish Anti-Piracy Group gave a speech. In this speech, Mr. Schluter espoused how much he loves child pornography. Why does he love child pornography so much?

"Child pornography is great! ...It is great because politicians understand child pornography. By playing that card, we can get them to act, and start blocking sites. And once they have done that, we can get them to start blocking file-sharing sites."

-Johan Schluter, Danish Anti-Piracy Group

Using this logic, intellectual property advocates have successfully played law enforcement agencies and politicians into their hands and have begun their blatant and unashamed attack on basic civil liberties.

What the IP lobbies never counted on was the counterpoint to call them on their nonsense. The Pirate movement is that counterpoint. We believe in building a future we can be proud of, rather than a future that is profitable for a few. The fundamental need for people to share has been a tenant of society since we first started drawing on cave walls. The IP lobby successfully shut down mainstream commercial sharing with Napster and Kazaa, but also succeeded in helping the proliferation of more underground methods of sharing like the Bit-torrent protocol.

People will always find ways to share and communicate, whether it moves to unregulated darknets that pop in and out of existence in hours or we resort back to sneakernet dead-drops. Seizing property without a warrant and trying to extend a single government's jurisdiction around the world only succeeds in infringing on basic civil liberties.

An industry that has to suspend civil liberties to make money is an industry the world needs to be without.

THE PARABLE OF THE PASTURE
HOWARD DENSON

This parable is probably a hundred years old, but its meaning is as fresh and significant today as it ever was:

> "The voters are like cattle in a pasture. Every
> four years, someone brings a bull around and
> lets it loose in the field. It doesn't matter
> which bull they send in because the same thing
> happens to the cows."

You may supply the moral of the story in language that suits your sense of propriety today.

Back in the 1960s and early 70s, George Wallace repeatedly said that there wasn't a dime's worth of difference between the Republicans and the Democrats. Actually back then there probably was a quarter's difference.

I think it was Richard Neustadt who made the point a few years earlier that, if you take away just a few issues from the Democratic and then Republican members of Congress, you truly would have a very homogenous body of politicians.

No Safe Harbor

In recent years, we have watched as Barack Obama campaigned on change, change, change, and then the Tea Party contingent campaigned on throwing all the rascals out and making real change.

I will argue that, as time goes on, whoever is claiming to advocate change will end up supporting the status quo. The Tea Party members have joined movements that want their elected officials to serve a term – okay, maybe two – and then go home.

Some individuals may (reluctantly?) do their terms and then resign, but it is more common for a transformation to occur as the outsider morphs into an insider. Politician A sees all the good that he or she is doing and decides that it would be best for him or her to run again, by golly, in order to do more good.

We humans always wrap our motives and intentions in the flag or the Bible: "America needs folks like me in Washington. God wants me there to make sure that this stays a Christian country." We claim we don't want bribes or the more usual equivalent, campaign donations. We can't be bought, but, by gum, we do look after folks who think like us. This billion-dollar airplane isn't needed, the Pentagon doesn't even want it, but we've got to defend America and keep the plants making parts for the good of the country, the state, our district, and (of course, this is not important) our buddies.

We like to look back to the marble days of our country when the Founding Fathers, with halos around their head, complained about King George III, and the tariffs, and the taxes. There's one problem: We don't like to think that our forefathers often were driven by profit as much as principle.

As the party system evolved, our forefathers passed sedition laws to shut up the unpatriotic loud-mouths in the other party. First Amendment rights? Not for traitors. They deserve a hanging or at least a good hoss-whipping. We'll compromise with a good tarring-and-feathering.

When the federal government needed money, the early fathers listened to Alexander Hamilton and established the Second National Bank, run by Nicholas Biddle. All of the government revenue in this young country was concentrated in his bank, and it didn't take long for this hard-working financier to begin thinking of the revenue as his money.

Unfortunately, he ran afoul of Andy Jackson, who, in retrospect, could have run on the slogan "It's time for a real psycho for President." Jackson's stubbornness helped to derail Biddle's attempts to blackmail the U.S. and eventually to destroy his house of cards.

Across the pond over a century earlier, England saw a big abuse with its "South Sea Bubble," a scheme for a company to take on the nation's debt and then pay it off with special deals. It didn't work thanks to Graft and its kissing cousins Inefficiency and Ineptitude.

During the Good War of the 20th Century, Americans remembered Pearl Harbor and rallied together. Some sang "Glory Glory Hallelujah" as they envisioned the millions of dollars that Washington was spending throughout the country. Did local contractors do right by their country and give the best deals on building new military bases? Of course, not. They worked on a "cost-plus" system.

The Truman Committee revealed that they were jacking up the prices. Suddenly it was costing twice what they normally charged to build a barracks or a PX. Senator Harry and Bess hopped into their old Dodge and drove to these military sites to see if building materials were actually there, if workers were sawing two-by-fours and installing plumbing or foundations. Truman also looked into the dollar-a-year moguls who were supposedly helping in the war effort. Often they weren't; instead, they were trashing competitors and trying to use the feds to weaken or destroy employees' union.

In fact, any time the government has accumulated millions or billions in a special fund, corruption has ensued. Let's take the case of the Bureau of Indian Affairs (as summarized by the online Monitor.net):

> "An 1887 law made the federal government responsible for collecting fees from anyone who uses tribal land, with the money to be held in a trust fund. Billions were paid by mining companies, ranchers, and others over the decades; currently over $300 million is collected annually by the BIA (Bureau of Indian Affairs), part of the Interior Dept. The money was supposed to be given to the descendants of the original Indian land owners, but every audit since 1928 has found billions missing from the trust fund. It is certainly the greatest financial scandal in the history of the United States.

> "In 1996, a class-action suit against the BIA was filed. The feds delayed, often claiming that vital records couldn't be found. It was later discovered that boxes of documents were being destroyed even as lawyers from the government said they were searching for them. In 1999, Interior Secretary Bruce Babbitt, BIA head Kevin Gover, and Treasury Secretary Robert Rubin were cited for contempt of court, and Rubin and Babbitt were fined $625,000 each. In April 2000, the Interior Department moved record keeping operations from New Mexico to Virginia, where officials

said all information would be entered into a
master computer program [price tag of $40
million]. Critics accused Washington of more
stalling, charging that there was no proof that
the computer worked as promised." [1]

It didn't.

It may be pointless to argue how much of the BIA revenue was
simply stolen. At a minimum, it's fair to say that it provides an
excellent example of robbing Peter to pay Paul; revenue seldom
went to the Native Americans but was diverted into the general
fund.

That ploy has been used with the Social Security monies, as
patriots say it's a shame to just have that money sit there; let's
use it for things we need now; we'll even stick in IOU's each
time we take out some cash.

Now fine patriots want to turn over future Social Security
monies to the private sector, to the guys and gals who brought
us the musical extravaganza "The Big Meltdown of 2008."
Remember the hit songs? "A Shaft for You and a Golden
Parachute for Me," "We're Too Big to Fail, But You'll Pay and
Say What the Hell," "A Bonus and a Bail-Out, and Another
Bonus for Me." And the grand finale, "Two, Four, Six, Eight –
Let's All De-regulate."

All of that, of course, brings up the matter of China. When they
were pitching social protestors in jail, it was uncomfortable.
Only Hitler, Stalin, and their own Mao would approve of such
brutality. By and by, however, we read about their lining up a
corrupt businessman or politico against a wall and shooting
him. Rough, but perhaps justified.

No Safe Harbor

In our own country, some high-fliers in business have crossed the line from merely being crooks to being traitors to their country and fellow citizens. The late Ken Lay of Enron infamy and Bernie Madoff of Ponzi infamy are two candidates who would not have thrived indefinitely in China.

We have to go back 2,000 years to Ovid to see why the American establishment will tolerate crooks in high places:

> "Treason doth never prosper: what's the reason?
> Why if it prosper, none dare call it treason."

And the taxpayers remained in their pastures, patiently chewing their cud and wondering what's going to happen next.

[This essay appeared in its original format on the author's website, http://howarddenson.webs.com/apps/blog/]

INDIE AUTHORS SHAKING THE PILLARS OF PUBLISHING
REAGEN DANDRIDGE DESILETS

Over the last few years, the publishing world has begun to drastically change. As with the music industry in recent times, people are beginning to no longer need large firms to get published. With the rise of the ebook and print-on-demand services, a writer can now circumvent the traditional system and release their work directly to the public themselves. Indie writers like John Locke, who have sold over 1 million ebooks this year without an agent or publisher, have really begun to raise some eyebrows. There are writers, like Nina Paley, who have had great success publishing without leaning on copyright laws, and, recently, liberty activist and author Tarrin P. Lupo holds the top rated book on Amazon Kindle in the Historical Fiction for his novel, *Pirates of Savannah*. This kind of success was unheard of until just a few years ago. With all the available resources online for helping authors self-publish, as well as the ability to engage in social networking, these new authors are able to compete with the large publishing firms unlike ever before.

There are a lot of methods to self-publish, but how difficult is it really and what are some of the issues, and risks and rewards of putting oneself out there? There isn't a right or wrong in this – as mentioned, there are very successful self-published authors and there are others that don't make it so well. Some issues that can hamper an author are lack of editing, the wrong cover art and improper formatting; however, social and local networking are great ways to find people that have the know-how and skill to help with those concerns. There are several services to choose from to print books as well as services to create all the formats needed to sell ebooks. But, what are some of the unseen obstacles that current and potential self-published authors face on a regular basis? How does it impact the very idea of free press and free speech?

One of the first things that are needed by an author to self-publish is an International Standard Book Number, better known as an ISBN. It's not required in some cases with ebooks but to maximize your sales and get listed in large name distributors and retailers, an author really does need one. In order to get one, the author has to go to the only company allowed to sell them in the United States, Bowker. I suppose the idea is that it is easier to have one company managing the numbers, but a closer look reveals that, as usual, a monopoly creates a stifling environment that encourages price gouging and poor customer service. Self-publishing authors face expenses that can be very draining, especially in regards to getting one or more skilled editors. However, when the author goes to purchase an ISBN in preparation for publishing, they discover that one single number is $125.00! And to add to that, if the author intends to sell in print and in ebook forms, then they will need two separate numbers for the same title. Granted, the more numbers one can buy at once, the lower the cost of each number, but if someone has a hard time coming up with the money for a single number then the idea of buying in bulk becomes daunting. In the world of self-publishing, one can get ISBNs relatively inexpensively from others that buy in bulk, such as the aforementioned printing and ebook companies online, but they usually restrict how and where you can sell since they are in a sense, the "publisher". It is possible to find others in the field of self-publishing that have been able to get large numbers of ISBNs in bulk and they are willing to sell at a much reduced rate as well. However, they may or may not have the distributing restrictions that the other companies do. There is a chance that anyone providing ISBNs as the publishing imprint would be held liable for something printed, so they will have the option to, essentially, censor what they choose to allow.

This entire process is draining and discouraging to those that wish to publish and it is not necessary. It is not unreasonable that a free market would agree to use and maintain the option for a standard of numbers to increase sales avenues. An example of this is in the world of computers (please note, it's not a truly free market, but this is an example of how we can see it work). The personal computer is an open source product that can be built by a manufacturer or by someone with the know how in their own home. It can be loaded with software built by a variety of companies and it can also be run on open source operating systems with the ability for the user to change the code and republish for use by others. The other option is the Mac, which is severely closed source and leaves the user with little options for variety and customization. Mac does a good job making up for it, but in the end, it's not enough. There are rises in compatible software so that a basic "standard" can be more easily achieved, improving their own chances on the market.

So why isn't there another option to purchase ISBNs? Because the government granted the monopoly. Clearly, this presents a problem with the idea of "freedom of the press" and indeed, "freedom of speech" as well. Perhaps, with the emergence of a large number of self-publishing authors, it would be best if the government stepped aside and allowed the market to regulate itself. This would help loosen the burden on potential authors and publishers and allow this avenue to be more open and available.

There are other things for the self-published author to consider as well and that is the idea of "intellectual property." The common theme is that the author retains all rights (and illustrator and commentators if such is included in the book). There are some real questions about whether or not intellectual property laws really protect the authors, artists, musicians, etc. A common question is "Did William Shakespeare suffer any income loss without the protection of intellectual property and copyright laws?" Since we are still reading and creating with the use of his works centuries later, it would appear not. Would he want the use and adaptation of his works reduced for the idea of gaining permission from a publishing agent or company first? Well, that answer can't be known but it is hard to imagine he would have wanted his works contained and restricted.

Another example for modern times is the cancellation of the series *Firefly*. The original network, FOX, aired it poorly and it wasn't received very well as a result. However, the show's creator, artists, actors and writers didn't give up, and soon after, the movie *Serenity* was released. The 'franchise' continues to grow, more than half a decade later on the steam of fans, unwilling to let such a good idea die with FOX's refusal to release or sell rights to it. How is FOX protecting those that put in their blood, sweat, and tears by doing this? They aren't. Plain and simple.

So what are some other options that authors can take if they so choose? Here are some ideas:

1. Creative Commons – CC is a comfortable jumping board for most people wanting to get away from the stifling world of copyright laws. The author/artist can better control how their work is shared and it is legit in the eyes of the law. See more at http://creativecommons.org/

2. Copyleft – Copyleft is a broad term used to describe anything but copyright.

3. Copyheart – Copyheart is one way you can label your work to show love and appreciation. See more at http://copyheart.org/

4. Anti-copyright – Anti-copyright fully embraces the notion that ideas themselves cannot be owned. It is NOT permission to plagiarize (to understand the difference, please see http://blog.ninapaley.com/2011/06/27/credit-is-due/). For more information and a complete definition of Anti-copyright, see http://anticopyright.com/

Why would any of this matter in a society where established publishing firms go to great lengths to get well written, edited and printed material on the market? Why wouldn't it? Ours is a country that believes so much in the importance of free speech that it was the very first amendment to the Constitution of the United States, whose ratification was delayed because it didn't specifically protect liberties. The very first amendment of the Bill of Rights states:

"Congress shall make no law respecting an establishment of religion, or prohibiting the free exercise thereof; or abridging the freedom of speech, or of the press; or the right of the people peaceably to assemble, and to petition the Government for a redress of grievances."

The Bill of Rights strived to accomplish naming the liberties that were natural-born rights to be protected (as opposed to "rights" only granted by man or paper) and one of the most important was the freedom of speech and press. "Press" refers to the printing press and not only newspapers and journalists. The U.S. Supreme Court's ruling in Lovell v. City of Griffin, GA, 303 U.S. 444 (1938) agrees that it includes anything published. So, the appearance of a lot of new authors that are self-publishing is a huge boost to the idea of "Freedom of the Press" and very much a boost to the American lifestyle and culture.

No Safe Harbor

In conclusion, authors have a lot more resources available to help them self-publish, even more than is initially seen on the surface. Be open to new avenues and ideas, take a deep breath, and embrace the leap of faith that it can be done!

BREAKING THE TWO PARTY TWO-STEP
ANDREW "K'TETCH" NORTON

The first Tuesday in November is election day. It is a day when people all over the country go out, and exercise democracy. In some countries, the very act of voting is seen as a triumph, something worthwhile to be attained. The US sees it as so important, that several countries have been invaded in the past century for the purposes of restoring democracy, yet the US does not have a functioning democracy itself, instead there is a pseudo-democracy, where only two parties are allowed to participate, much like in the most restrictive countries; China, Algeria, North Korea.

There are several myths about elections and voting, and I'm going to try and dispel them, or at least explain why what seems like such a good theory, doesn't work out in practice. I'm going to focus on US politics, but much of this holds true for other countries using a first-past-the-post (FPTP) system, such as the UK. In addition, I'll use the term "Major Parties" or "Major Party" to collectively describe the Republicans and Democrats. It's not an ideal choice of term, but it is one in common use in state laws across the country when talking about ballot access, to refer to those parties.

No Safe Harbor
If you vote for a third party, you're wasting your vote.

There is a never ending stream of partisan rhetoric when it comes to third parties. One of the most common claims is that voting for a 3rd party candidate is 'a wasted vote'. It has led to the rise of tactical voting in the US, where instead of voting for the person they want (if they are not one of the big two parties) we have people voting for the 'big 2' representative they dislike least. This was best exemplified in the 2004 US Presidential elections, when people who hated Bush voted for Kerry, and those that hated Kerry voted for Bush. What went completely unnoticed was the third choice in almost every state - that of the Libertarian Party and Michael Badnarik (he was not on the ballot in New Hampshire, or Oklahoma), or for that matter, the Green Party, who were on the ballot in about half the states.

This 'tactical voting' is the waste of a vote. Instead of voting for the person you wish to represent you, you are voting to try and deny someone else from doing so, by supporting the opponent who is believed to be the greatest challenge. This then leads to the two major parties producing candidates who are at odds with each other, to get this dichotomy, and play people into an 'us or them' situation.

There is another cost. The elected representatives in Congress are universally distrusted, and often thought of as corrupt. Why? Well, they don't actually represent the views of their constituents. What they represent is the views of the political party of the candidate that was not as disliked as the other. The other result is the rise in negative campaign adverts. Why spend money saying "vote for me, I'm better," when you can spend the money pointing out how bad your major opponent is, and get the tactical vote as a response. The additional bonus from this method is if you lose, you've got your adverts to say "I told you so," and if you win you've got very few promises to be held accountable for.

All this from tactical voting. What a sham!

United States Pirate Party

Third parties are a waste of time. They will never win.

There is no reason why they are a waste of time. The main reason they won't win is not because people don't support them, but due to tactical voting (see above) people are too afraid to be on the losing side. In addition, there are other elements to supporting the party that matches your views most closely, even if it's a 3rd party. Aside from winning the election, there are other goals that can be achieved, such as federal funding if the party reached 5% in the previous election. This can be a substantial benefit to many candidates. Major parties are also scared of third parties. In 2004, when the Libertarian party sued the Commission for Presidential Debates (the organization that runs the presidential campaign debates), the Republican party, and the Democratic Party, over being unfairly excluded from the debates (they had a nationally available candidate, and the debate was paid for using state funds, and held in a state venue (Arizona State university for the 3rd debate), the debate could have gone ahead if the two candidates had agreed to allow Badnarik to participate. Both refused. The Presidential Debates are a substantial piece of advertising, rather than actual debate when it excludes significant candidates. Ninety minutes of prime time television and radio is expensive, and when you add in the news coverage and analysis of it, it's a major chunk.

One estimate is that the debates work out to be worth at least $40 million in advertising. That's a substantial sum, and would be more than the total campaign budgets of the minor parties, much less the independents. Of course, $40 million is a drop in the bucket compared to the spending nationally on Major Party candidates, but the desire to control is one that tends to override any mere cost. And costs are something the 2010 election has in spades. In 2008, $2.5 billion was spent. For 2010, a mid-term election (which is traditionally less costly than a presidential election year), it's estimated that between $3 billion and $4 billion was spent on campaign advertising, almost certainly focused on the two main parties.

On the other side of the fence, minor party candidates are often asked why they even bother. Again, in 2004, at the Libertarian Party Conference, Michael Badnarik addressed this very issue, saying

"As a Libertarian candidate, I frequently face the 'wasted vote' syndrome. People tell me that I'm a good candidate. They believe in what I stand for, but they can't bring themselves to vote for me because they don't want to waste their vote. If you were in prison, and you had a 50% chance of lethal injection, a 45% chance of going to the electric chair, and only a 5% chance of escape, are you likely to vote for lethal injection because that is your most likely outcome? Your survival depends on voting for escape even if that's only a 5% chance."

Escape is, of course, voting *for* what you believe in, rather than the death of voting against yourself, voting "tactically."

Again, it's down to tactical voting. The perception that 3rd parties won't win, because voting for them is a wasted vote. Because it's a wasted vote, people don't vote for them. Thus they don't win. This validates people's view that they were right not to vote for them. It's a self-fulfilling prophecy. It's one that must be broken, in order to bring some actual democracy to the government.

Voting the party ticket

A lot of times, people will vote a straight ticket. That means that people will vote for every Democrat, or every Republican on the ballot. The theory is that the party represents the voters point of view, and so voting a straight ticket is the best, easiest way to vote their view.
It's not that simple though. If it were simply a measure of the party position, then why do we need candidates? Just assign a block vote to the party's national committee chairman. It also completely negates the

need for primaries. If the party affiliation is all that's needed, why is a publicly funded primary needed? All the candidates on the primary ballot represent the party, so they should all stand for the same thing.

We all know that candidates differ widely on what they represent, which is why the whole concept of a "straight ticket vote" is so horrific. That people vote for a candidate, for their representation, without looking at the candidates and what they stand for relying instead on a small letter placed next to their name, is insulting to the concepts of democracy, and insulting to the candidates. It trivializes them and means they're nothing more than a mouthpiece.

Of course, if candidates wish to just be a mouthpiece for a national chairman, then they're not a good choice as a candidate anyway. The idea of a candidate is to represent their constituents in the government, with a party providing support and guidance and a basic direction. These days, candidates are representing the major parties to the constituents.

There is nothing wrong with voting for candidates of different parties. If the candidate's position matches your views, then you should vote for them irrespective of their party affiliation.

The 1992 Eddie Murphy film The Distinguished Gentleman played on this premise, the "dumb voter" syndrome. Instead of a party though, he went for a name, but it's the same principle. Voters went in without knowledge (or care) and just looked for something vaguely familiar, be it a surname, or a party affiliation.

sigh

Taken altogether, it's a sad situation, producing terrible results. It's why we need electoral reform, in order to restore a government that focuses on policies, rather than attacking others because of party identification, and trying to prevent new parties entering and participating on an even keel – that would be too democratic, and upset the status quo.

Before you vote, do your homework, check who your candidates are, and what they stand for, and above all else, please, VOTE BASED ON THE CANDIDATES AND WHAT YOU STAND FOR. This is your government you are electing, it's not *American Idol*, or some other pointless, inconsequential TV show. It's as real, and as serious as it gets. For all that people go on about illegal immigrants, those who were lucky enough to be born citizens, act as a complete disgrace when they abuse the privilege of citizenship.

The real solution would be to adopt proportional representation in some form. It's considered "too complex" for Americans to understand, yet countries like France and Mexico seem to have no problem with it.

And above all else, don't complain about the government you get, if you voted tactically, dismissed candidates because of their party, chose not to vote, or just voted a straight ticket. It's your fault, and the fault of those that acted like you, and has been since this country was founded. Next time, use your brain instead - your country will thank you.

It's your vote, make it count!

FLUID DEMOCRACY
WILLIAM SIMS BAINBRIDGE

Worldwide, Internet-based social computing is creating entirely new political realities (Howard 2011). In Germany, there is much discussion of *Liquid Democracy*, innovative forms of representation far more flexible than those we have become accustomed to. The phrase "liquid democracy" belongs to the English language, not the German, and it is not uncommon for one language to borrow from another. Often, word meanings are shifted slightly in the process, as for example some Europeans abbreviate *software* as *soft*, because they use quite another word for the meaning of the English word *soft*. The automatic translation website FreeTranslation.com renders *Liquid Democracy* into German as *Flüssige Demokratie*, and *Flüssige Demokratie* into English as *Fluid Democracy*. Liquid metaphors are quite common in electronics and computer talk, such as *streaming video*, *electric current*, *wave*. I prefer the term *fluid democracy* because it makes clear that the fluctuating property of liquids is most salient for the discussion.

This essay is a reconnaissance of the technical means available for revolutionizing the political process, using advanced information technology to develop a new alternative to both representative democracy and direct democracy. In the forms of representative democracy prevalent in post-industrial societies today, all too often the elected representatives become captives of wealthy interest groups, rather than really representing the people, or become frozen into outdated ideological positions. Direct democracy presents the danger that the general public will be deceived about the nature of societal problems, whether by distortions broadcast through mass media or by their own wishful thinking, and make foolish decisions, even impulsively changing course so quickly that no progress is made in any direction. Problems that afflict both extreme forms of system include how to protect the right of minorities, how to incorporate professional expertise in political decision making, and how to find responses to new situations that have yet to be defined for popular opinion.

The point is not to jettison political traditions merely out of fascination with novelty, but to find better ways of satisfying the needs of the public for progressive, responsive government, under conditions of rapid cultural and economic change. It is obvious to everyone that the governments of advanced nations have in fact been functioning poorly, and some kind of major redesign is sorely needed. However, this does not mean that the designers of traditional systems were fools, and in fact there is much to learn from them.

A widely understood example is the difficulty of finding the right balance between stability and rapid response, which, for example, the creators of the national legislatures of the United States basically understood. The House of Representatives is elected every two years, from districts with approximately equal population, and thus responds more directly and more quickly to trends in popular opinion. Senators serve for six years, about a third facing the electorate every two years, but representing geographic areas with unequal populations having their own semi-independent political systems. The point is not that this system is ideal, but that it recognizes the design issue of stability versus rapidity of response. When we develop new Internet systems for achieving what has been called Liquid Democracy, using a very different set of innovative institutions, we still need to face this issue.

Thus, one example of a design feature that needs to be built into the new system is a feedback mechanism that carefully speeds up or slows down the rate of change, to achieve a dynamic balance appropriate for the rate of change in external conditions, and for the distance to a social goal that needs to be achieved.

Another example is how to balance privacy with accountability. A classic example is the secret ballot, in which the voters know whom they are voting for, but the politicians do not know how individual citizens voted. In more complex systems, finding the right balance can be a real challenge, for example concerning government employees. How can citizens doing business with the government be assured they are being treated fairly, while respecting a degree of privacy for government employees? How can responsible whistle-blowers call attention to problems without endangering their careers? These questions will become acute as we move toward new political systems, facilitated by modern communication technologies, in which many people are constantly shifting roles, being a common citizen at one point in time, a political leader at a second point in time, and a valued worker carrying a public responsibility at a third point. We cannot establish immutable design principle now for the political systems of the future, but we must constantly consider issues like these as we move forward through a period of innovation and experiment.

Current Events

A good starting point is the statement by the Liquid Democracy Squad of the Berlin Pirate Party, a group of about two dozen members who discussed the possibilities from September 30, 2009, until March 24, 2010. Their key idea was this:

> Each participant can decide how far he wants to shoulder his own interests, or how far he wants to be represented by others. In particular, he may at any time reclaim his delegated voting right, and this does not have to wait until a new election period.

This results in a network of delegations that is constantly in flux. [URL 1]

As conceptualized by the Berlin group, an individual has considerable liberty to determine how he or she would be represented. With respect to tax law, the person may select political Party A as the representative, while for environmental policy selecting Party B. Instead of a party, the person may select another individual. And these decisions can be changed at any time.

It is easy to imagine how this could be handled online. Each person would have a private page inside a password-protected governmental database. It would list some moderate number of areas of government decision making, with the option after each to select registered political parties from a drop-down menu, or to insert the name and unique ID number of another individual person. The database would constantly tabulate support for each party in each topic area, calculating weighting variables to calibrate the relative power of that party to decide the next specific vote in that area. Thus a party's strength in Parliament would be decided not by how many of its politicians had won seats in the most recent election, but by the momentary fraction of the electorate that had selected it to represent them on the particular issue at hand.

In cases when Voter A delegated to Voter B, there are two possibilities. First, Voter A's party choice could copy Voter B's party choice, changing whenever Voter B changed a party selection. Second, if Voter B achieves some threshold number of delegations from other voters, Voter B could become in effect an independent member of Parliament. The balance between party influence in Parliament, versus the influence of individual delegates representing many people but without a party organization, could change over time and across issues. In addition, each voter might have several selection pages in the secure online database, one for local government, one for regional government, one for national government, and ideally even one for world government.

Presumably, each political party, and each unaligned individual delegate, would have a public web page listing positions on the various general issues. It is conceivable that some party or solo delegate might choose to communicate privately, even in secret, with individual voters, and no technical barrier prohibits this. However, democracy generally benefits from broad public discussion, and this system assumes that some kind of public debate has identified what the distinct issue areas are. It is one thing to say that tax policy is logically separate from environmental policy, but when a decision must be made about taxing emissions from a polluting industry, the picture becomes complex.

When it comes time to implement Liquid Democracy, there will be a host of very specific technical questions, including many about the processes used to identify opinion leaders and topic areas. The simple idea just presented of a government database with a private page for each voter is only one of many possible ways to proceed, and a modern political system may require combining several of them. Furthermore, we have not considered yet how a political party would develop its platform, and we should imagine how advanced information technology might manage that difficult process. Without pretending at this early point to know which methods should be used in what combination, we can catalog possible components of a twenty-first century political system based on Internet.

Components

A very large number of information technology methods have been developed recently to support group decision making, and they can be assembled in different ways. Many of them have not generally been presented in political terms, so it will take some imagination even to recognize some of the valuable technological resources available to us. Here we shall consider only three: reputation systems, recommender systems, and online group formation systems.

From a certain perspective, Google is a political entity, ruling world culture by deciding where people will find the information they desire, in terms of the most complex classification system that has ever existed, and a dynamic one at that. It is political because it is based on the equivalent of voting, in the form of links people put on their web pages to other people's pages. Without getting into details, the Google search engine uses two kinds of data. One is the words written on a web page, and the other is the pattern of links coming to a web page. A key part of the mechanism is the *pagerank algorithm* - actually a class of algorithms that assign a score to each web page in terms of the links coming to it, adjusted by the ranks of the pages that sent those links (Page et al 1998; [URL 2]).

For example, consider the English-language Wikipedia page of Pirate Parties International. To find many of the web pages that have links to this particular page, one can enter into Google: "link:en.wikipedia.org/wiki/Pirate_Parties_International." On October 21, 2011, Google listed 141 such pages, including some belonging to branches of the party, as well as pages in many different languages. Entering "link:www.piratenpartei.de/" turns up fully ten times as many web pages. It is even possible to enter two "link:" URLs, and get a listing of all the pages that link to both of the two target webpages, which can become a metric of how similar those two pages are, in comparison with other pairs of pages that might have more or fewer common in-coming links.

Thus Google page rank is first of all a measure of popularity, but also data that can be used to map web pages in terms of similarity. Of course we should be cautious about using Google as our voting system. Yes, one can easily tabulate the relative numbers of in-coming links for the web pages of politicians, but this is not the same thing as their popularity with voters. Many of the highly ranked pages sending links may belong to ideological organizations, venial corporations, or crazy fanatics who put up many webpages that draw attention for being bizarre, not for being wise. Yet as a technical method akin to a voting system, the Google search engine has been remarkably successful and may have lessons for those who wish to reform the political system in the light of advanced communication technology.

In a sense, Google is a *reputation system*, and its methods can be adopted to measure the reputations of political leaders, or to cluster them into parties if they have not already organized. The original area in which such network-based techniques were developed was bibliometrics - specifically studying the pattern of literature citations to identify the most influential publications and scientists (Börner 2010; 2011). Similar methods are now used in a number of fields, using a range of computational methods, to identify leaders in a network of communication.

A *recommender system* is a database and statistical analysis engine that recommends future actions to the user - typically what movies to rent or books to buy - based on the user's prior behavior or expressed preferences (Basu et al 1998; Canny 2002; Herlocker et al 2004). These systems are widely used in Internet advertising, in order to customize the sales effort to fit the interests of the audience, but can be developed not only to cluster small issues into coherent political programs, but also even to conduct a form of science-moderated direct voting. The distinction between reputation systems and recommender systems is unclear, and the two share many technical features. But the best way to get the idea across is to look at one of the best-known pure recommender systems, the Netflix movie rating system. [URL 3]

After people rent a movie from Netflix, they are encouraged to rate it on a preference scale from 1 to 5, and their responses are used to determine which movies Netflix will recommend they should rent. Starting in 2006, Netflix held a contest, providing a huge training subset of their data, based on hundreds of thousands of raters, and challenging contestants to devise an algorithm that would best predict customers' ratings on movies for which the data were not in the training set. I entered the contest, not intending to compete, but to explore how such data might be used to map the styles and ideological orientations of movies. I knew from my earlier research, that people's preferences were often largely shaped by the visual style of a movie, the leading actors in it, and the year in which it was released - but modulo all these extraneous factors ideology could sometimes be detected (Bainbridge 1992: 470-481, 2007).

To illustrate the methods here, I have selected 15 movies that concern artificial intelligence or virtual realities - topics close to fluid democracies in their reliance on information technology for radical social purposes. One consequence is that these films may not differ much from each other in term of ideologies, precisely because they have so much in common. The first methodological challenge is that many respondents rate very few movies, so to get robust results I focused on the 6,551 respondents who had rated at least 10 of the 15, only 110 of whom had rated all 15. They are all diehard sci-fi fans, but if the data concerned politics rather than films, we would be dealing with knowledgeable experts on that very different topic. Table 1 lists the films, the year each was released, the average ratings, and the results of a factor analysis of the data.

Table 1: Fifteen Movies about Advanced Information Technology

Title	Year	Netflix Raters	Mean Netflix Rating (1-5)	Factor 1	Factor 2	Factor 3	Factor 4
Blade Runner	1982	6313	4.18	0.84			
The Matrix	1999	6523	4.56	0.70			
The Terminator	1984	6468	4.25	0.70			
Tron	1982	5563	3.58	0.62			
Westworld	1973	3173	3.50	0.54	0.55		
RoboCop	1987	5914	3.55	0.46	0.46		
eXistenZ	1999	2498	3.07		0.77		
Star Trek: The Motion Picture	1979	5321	3.46		0.70		
The Thirteenth Floor	1999	2524	3.31		0.60	0.51	
Bicentennial Man	1999	4658	3.27			0.83	
A.I. Artificial Intelligence	2001	5990	3.14			0.69	
I, Robot	2004	6047	3.81			0.41	0.56
Cyborg	1989	2068	2.79				0.66

Johnny Mnemonic	1995	4189	3.03				0.52
2001: A Space Odyssey	1968	5920	3.81				-0.75

Four factors resulted, which may be considered four dimensions of variation across the films, or clusters that group together films with much in common. The number in the four factor columns are *loadings*, expressing how strongly each film represents the factor. Note the negative loading for 2001 in the last column, implying it has a quality opposite to that of the three other films in the category. The first factor seems to have clear meaning, grouping together very high quality, popular films with considerable intellectual depth. The fact that some clusters of films are hard to interpret suggests we may face a similar difficulty in the realm of politics. Note especially that the factors overlap, which is not common in factor analysis, but could easily be the case in a multi-party political system, in which the platforms of competing parties contained some of the same issues.

In earlier research, I had used the same methods to analyze science-fiction authors, finding not only that four dimensions of variation existed, but that each had extremely clear meaning (Bainbridge 1986). The first group of authors wrote hard-science fiction very closely connected to physical science and technology, and filled with optimism. The second group wrote new-wave fiction, closer to the social sciences, pessimistic, and critical of contemporary society. The third group wrote a variety of kinds of fantasy that ignore real science and emphasize magic. The fourth group consisted of pioneer writers like Jules Verne and H. G. Wells; indeed the fourth dimension of science fiction is time.

If the units being rated were politicians, some of the factors would be clear, representing central individuals in well-established parties. Some would be more complex, perhaps connecting politicians of whatever party who had an anarchist or isolationist streak. Some factors might be based on race, gender, or geographical area, and a few factors might be quite indeterminate in meaning. But if we had a recommender system for politicians, a person who already liked politicians A, B, and C, could be advised what other politicians that person might like, providing links to their websites so the person can check out their platforms and other writings. If the units being rated were specific political positions, then each factor would represent a reasonably coherent platform of compatible positions.

Especially for local politics, it is important to build into the mix of methods some that enable formation of groups of ordinary citizens to tackle particular problems of interest to them. Massively Multiplayer Online (MMO) games do this all the time, and some have excellent systems for short-term team building. For example, *World of Warcraft* has a good system for assembling small teams of five players, or even raids as big as 40, linking themselves through a real-time communication system on the basis of a short-term practical goal (Bainbridge 2010). When there are as many as 40 participants, the system is hierarchical, usually assembling individuals in realtime into 8 sub-groups of 5, with more intense communication among the leaders of these small groups, and from the momentary leadership down to ordinary members. The newer MMO, *Rift*, has successfully worked out methods to bring together similar numbers of people instantly, in a given local area under sudden attack, even without much communication, or at least exceedingly fluid communication.

Long-duration voluntary groups are also common, often called *guilds*. A guild called "Science" I created in April 2008 in *World of Warcraft* to organize the world's first major scientific conference held inside an MMO, is still in existence three and a half years later (Bohannon 2008;

Bainbridge 2010a). When I registered the guild inside *World of Warcraft*, I had the power to name each of a half dozen levels of membership, and use the guild-leader part of the interface to decide what powers each level would have. For example, I let all members above the first level recruit new members to the guild, but only very high-level members could promote someone to a higher rank. After the conference, reasonable discussions with the most active members transferred the leadership from me to a subgroup of them. Structurally, such guilds look like dictatorships or oligarchies, but any group of dissatisfied members can always start their own guild, so the nominal leaders of successful guilds are more like servants than kings, exerting great effort to satisfy the membership.

To outline the contours and establish ubiquity of such guilds, Table 2 provides some data about 3,676 members of the largest such group in the classic MMO, *EverQuest II*. Called Blackhawks, it is organized into the series of eight membership ranks given in the table. In *EverQuest II*, as in most MMOs, there is a set system of experience advancement, an objective status ladder based on successful completion of missions inside this virtual world. Currently, the levels of experience run from 1 to 90, but with levels above 80 available only to committed players who have annual subscriptions. The three factions listed have evaluative labels in *EverQuest II*, but can be thought of as geographic representation districts, because members of the Good faction come from one district of the virtual world; those in the Evil faction come from another, and the Neutrals can come from either district.

Table 2: Members of the Blackhawks Guild in *EverQuest II*

Rank	Number of Avatars	Mean Level of Experience	Percent in Good Faction	Percent in Neutral Faction	Percent in Evil Faction
Leader	9	45	0.0%	100.0%	0.0%
Council	40	67.1	40.0%	50.0%	10.0%
Captain	43	57.9	34.9%	41.9%	23.3%
Commander	32	74.9	18.8%	59.4%	21.9%
Senior Member	381	69.9	25.2%	43.3%	31.5%
Contributor	451	57.0	29.9%	41.9%	28.2%
Member	1166	30.4	29.5%	43.3%	27.2%
Recruit	1554	34.2	28.3%	42.6%	29.2%

An extensive literature exists on MMO guilds, and we cannot take the time here to discuss all the findings, or all the tools used by different MMOs to create and support these groups. However, one point deserves emphasis because it links to fluid democracy. The members of Blackhawks are not people but avatars of people. *EverQuest II* is the only current MMO that makes public which avatars link together through one player, although it does not reveal the real-world identity of the person playing that set of avatars. These 3,676 Blackhawks avatars belong to 1,782 game accounts, for an average of 2.06 virtual representatives per person. The Berlin group imagined that each person could behave almost as multiple persons, with one vote per political issue area. The system of multiple avatars in MMOs, suggests there might be several ways in which voters could become multifaceted, even earning extra votes through investing time and effort in the system.

The Blackhawks website indicates that a single person is Leader of the guild, but this person has nine avatars, three of which have reached level 90. The 40 avatars in the council represent 8 people, only two of which lack level-90 avatars, for an average of 5 avatars each. Captains and Commanders are also considered to be leaders. The 43 captains represent 19 accounts, while the 32 Commanders represent 23 accounts. The guild seems mostly to operate by consensus among the higher ranks, but we could imagine a system in which each top-ranked avatar had a vote, giving some people multiple votes. *EverQuest II* offers many ways in which an avatar may earn points for the guild to which the avatar belongs, chiefly completing difficult missions inside the virtual world, earning status points with the guild. The system by which Blackhawks promotes people is very well stated on the guild's website:

> Basic promotions happens based on length of service and amount of status earned. Once you have made your first forums post, the first promotion is to Member. The next title, Contributor, requires at least two full weeks in the guild and a minimum of 5000 earned status points (per character - alts do not inherit your main's rank!).

> Contributors and above may take advantage of guild perks like buying certain status items and rent/mount cost reductions. The next promotion, Senior Members, are veterans of the guild who have been here for 2 months and earned a minimum of 15,000 status points.

To be promoted to Commander - you can either be nominated by two of your peers or by someone of higher rank.

To become a Captain you need the nomination of two Captains or higher. ALL nominations are subject to Council/Guild Leader approval.

A Commander will have a limited number of guild abilities enabled. These will be specified at the time of promotion. Captains will have slightly more authority. All ranked position holders generally have to have been a member of the guild for at least two months and have accumulated at least 20000 guild status.

Council members will be selected from the ranks of Captain or via special appointment from the Guild Leader.

All promotional guidelines are subject to change at any time. On rare occasion a member may be promoted before meeting the criteria posted above. This is at the discretion of the guild leader. Occasionally, we may also hold elections if the number of nominated people is high.

The promotions process is, as a general rule, intentionally vague. We are not seeking members who aspire to become commanders and above for the sake of holding a title, or wielding authority. Instead, we seek those individuals who lead by example and action, show organizational and leadership skills and an overwhelming desire to help others. That is the best way to get promoted on our team. Help people who need it, take the initiative and host some events, show maturity and leadership by example. [URL 4]

As outlined by the Berlin group, Liquid Democracy allows citizens to decide from moment to moment who will represent them on what issues. Earlier we noted that it is important to build into the political system a stabilization adjustment that achieves a favorable balance between rapid change and consistency. One way to do this is to delay the effect of a vote, and let the voter rescind it instantly if the voter changes opinions, or to distribute voting dates across the population, for example letting a person cast new votes annually based on their own birthdays. But as the *EverQuest II* system suggests, a very different way of stabilizing the system is to award political leaders points for things they achieve for their constituents, and have these points degrade at a slow rate.

Values

Traditional sociology assumed that each viable culture possessed a set of relatively stable *values*, often described as widely shared goals for social action, supported by systems of *norms* that constituted institutions (Parsons and Shils 1951). From this traditional conception, any weakening of the values and norms led to what the French called *anomie*, but has also been called *cultural strain* and *social pathology* (Durkheim 1897; Merton 1938; Smelser 1962). Today this conception seems very naive, both because the conditions of life are changing rapidly, and because different groups in society experience them in radically different ways (Bainbridge 1994). However, governments require goals, so it is still worthwhile asking what the values of society might be at a given point in time, being ready for the answer that they are varied and changing.

Since the 1930s, public opinion polls have been used to chart general popular sentiments, as well as in very focused efforts to predict or understand particular elections. A more recent example is a battery of questions about government programs incorporated in the General Social Survey (GSS), a long-running questionnaire study of the American public, which I am especially familiar with because I managed funding for it in the mid-1990s and have frequently used the data in my own research. One item from that battery, concerning funding for the space program, is a useful, future-oriented item to consider here.

The GSS is administered by an interviewer in the respondent's home, and the interviewer would introduce the battery of items thus: "We are faced with many problems in this country, none of which can be solved easily or inexpensively. I'm going to name some of these problems, and for each one I'd like you to tell me whether you think we're spending too much money on it, too little money, or about the right amount." In 1973, fully 61.4 percent of the 1,430 respondents said too much was being spent on "the space exploration program," while 7.5 said too little was being spent, and 31.1 percent said the right amount was being invested. These results could be compared with other government programs, and with the responses for the space program in other years. In 2010, 37.7 percent felt too much was being spent on the space program, 17.2 percent said too little, and 45.1 percent felt the current investment was about right. Anyone who wants to explore these and any other results from the General Social Survey can do so online. [URL 5]

If these data were the basis of decision-making through direct democracy, the space program would have been shut down in 1973, but would be continued today. It is possible to weight data from the general public, to give some people more influence than others. For example educated people and those who score higher on tests of scientific knowledge favor the space program more. We have already seen how advocates of fluid democracy plan to identify and empower opinion leaders. However, there is a different but highly compatible approach, seeking to identify the general values served by some government program or policy decision, and measure how important those particular values are to the public at large, even if they do not currently understand the specific issue at hand. Then, professional experts would go through a similar but more complex process to decide how to achieve those goals.

No Safe Harbor

I chose the space program as my example, because years ago I did a pilot study to explore some of the methods needed (Bainbridge 1991). The inspiration was the intense experience of being at NASA's Jet Propulsion Laboratory at the time of the Challenger space shuttle disaster in 1986, and sharing the horror of all the people there who had dedicated their lives to space exploration. Lacking funding, I was in no position to survey the general public, but the rather knowledgeable students of Harvard University were available to serve as respondents. I administered two very different questionnaires. The first one consisted largely of open-ended questions, where respondents were encouraged to write a number of possible goals for the space program, and 1,007 students did so. Their responses were then typed into a computer, although classification was done manually because today's natural language clustering programs were not yet available.

The second questionnaire asked respondents to rate each of 125 different possible space goals, which had been derived from the first questionnaire, on a scale saying how good a reason each one was for continuing the space program. Because the data matrix for 125 variables x 125 variables x 894 respondents was too big for the social science statistical software available at the time, I wrote my own clustering program to extract the fundamental values being served by the space program as reflected in how the respondents grouped the items implicitly. For example, military values were distinct from scientific ones, which in turn were distinct from idealistic goals. This pilot study was reported in a book, which is now available online. [URL 6]

This process can be carried out very effectively online today. In 1999, a massive online questionnaire study sponsored by the National Geographic Society, called Survey 2000 (Witte, Amoroso, and Howard 2000; Bainbridge 2004), included an open-ended question I developed asking people to write a brief prediction about the year 2100: "Imagine the future and try to predict how the world will change over the next century. Think about everyday life as well as major changes in society, culture, and technology." About 20,000 people responded, and after considerable analysis of their written text, 2,000 formal questionnaire items resulted. I wrote them into a Windows-based computer program that anyone can use to explore their own conceptions of the future, freely available online. [URL 7] In connection with fluid democracy, this study suggests one way in which the general public can be polled to identify issues of concern to them, of course using a variety of open-ended questions appropriate for a range of policy areas, and even larger number of respondents than a mere 20,000.

While it is very important to develop a new political system that can adjust the balance between direct democracy and representative democracy, the decisions of legislatures are only one early stage in political decision making. The study of space goals can illustrate this. Table 3 lists 14 space goals, out of a preliminary list of 49, which clustered together correlationally as revealed by a factor analysis. The data came from a 1977 pilot study of 225 American voters who lived in the Seattle, Washington area, data collected with the able help of Richard Wyckoff who at that time was a graduate student. This was only a pilot study, and the 1986 study was more extensive, yet because it polled voters the 1977 study seems symbolically appropriate to use here. The factor loading for an item represents essentially the correlation between the item and the underlying but unmeasured concept that unites the group, so we can see that the fundamental idea focuses on human colonization of the solar system. The popularity of each item is the percent of voters calling it an extremely good or moderately good reason for supporting the space program.

Table 3: Visionary Space Exploration Goals

Benefit of the Space Program	Factor Loading	Popularity
Overpopulation on Earth can be solved by using the living space on other planets.	0.70	24.9%
Space travel will lead to the planting of human colonies on new worlds in space.	0.70	24.3%
Society has a chance for a completely fresh start in space; new social forms and exciting new styles of life can be created on other worlds.	0.66	24.0%
Raw materials from the moon and other planets can supplement the dwindling natural resources of the Earth.	0.63	50.9%
Our world has become too small for human civilization and for the human mind; we need the wide open spaces of the stars and planets to get away from the confines of our shrinking world.	0.59	17.6%
Spaceflight is necessary to ensure the survival of the human race against destruction by natural or man-made disaster.	0.57	25.6%
Human societies have always needed to expand in order to remain healthy; space is the only direction left for such expansion.	0.56	31.4%

We must go beyond the finite Earth into infinite space in order to continue economic growth without limit.	0.54	20.7%
Space hospitals put into orbit where there is no gravity will be able to provide new kinds of medical treatment and give many patients easier recoveries.	0.53	50.70%
Commercial manufacturing can be done in space without polluting the Earth; completely new materials and products can be made in space.	0.47	40.6%
Communication with intelligent beings from other planets would give us completely new perceptions of humanity, new art, philosophy, and science.	0.44	55.3%
We can conduct certain dangerous kinds of scientific experiment far in space so accidents and other hazards will not harm anyone.	0.42	36.2%
Without spaceflight we would be trapped, closed-in, jailed on this planet.	0.41	14.7%
Rockets developed for spaceflight will be used for very rapid transportation of people, military equipment, or commercial goods over long distances on the Earth.	0.38	49.1%

From the perspective of a third of a century later, these 14 goals may seem even more fanciful than they did in 1977. Certainly none of them have been achieved, and a recent retrospective on my old study implies that the goals that could have been achieved, given humanity's technical capabilities, have been achieved, and we completely lack the technology for colonization of the solar system (Bainbridge 2009a). Many of the goals were relatively unpopular in 1977, but all of them touch on hopes for humanity that many future-oriented, thoughtful people hold. Today, the government of the United States is deadlocked about what the National Aeronautics and Space Administration should achieve beyond the confines of Earth.

I have argued that the funding should go entirely into fundamental research in science and engineering, that will increase our knowledge about the universe and perhaps prepare the way for much more advanced space technologies in future decades, and the manned space program should be halted (Bainbridge 2009b). However, any politician who advocates this position is likely to lose votes, because many people in the general public like the idea of human spaceflight, but lack the technical understanding to know how little we can accomplish at the present time.

Knowing what segments of the public want does not directly tell us how to give it to them, nor does it help us weigh the costs, against the costs and benefits of other goals the public also desires. The fluid network method described earlier, and already worked out in its general principles by leading thinkers in the worldwide Pirate Party, should be fully successful for many issues, but a second method with which we already have a good deal of experience is also worth considering. Indeed, the best approach may be a flexible mixture of the two methods. The second method I have in mind is *peer review* used by many scientific publications and science-funding agencies. It may be especially suitable when the public goals present difficult technical challenges that require unusually solid expertise that requires a considerable period of time to establish.

Expertise

The general public often conceptualizes the political process only in terms of elections and the functioning of legislatures, yet much of the real decision making is done inside government agencies where the processes are obscure by nature and intentionally hidden from public view. Major exceptions to this lack of transparency are many science-funding agencies of technically advanced nations. In particular, the *scientific peer review process* involves a very large number of experts, who are not government employees but teaching in universities or occasionally working in other technical settings. The use of these methods could be expanded, at the same time that fluid democracy was introduced into the electoral and legislative processes, to make proper use of expert knowledge that is too specialized or complex for the general public to understand.

Here is one of the ways a contemporary science agency can manage the peer review process (Bainbridge 2011). I will describe it in somewhat idealized terms, and not all of the features exist in any particular case; however all of these features are common.

In the course of human scientific development, new areas open up, and a sense develops in the relevant scientific community that funding should be devoted to research in one or another of them. In a somewhat chaotic process, individuals and small groups of colleagues may write *white papers*, outlining the potential of a new area. A science funding agency may then fund a series of small workshops, or even a major conference, to work out a scientific agenda for the early stages of exploration of the area. If the output of all this communication is promising, a new funding initiative is announced, with funds devoted to it either from several related existing programs or from a central fund of the agency. A formal funding announcement or *solicitation* is posted on the web, with a particular deadline date for submission usually set a few months after the posting to give academic researchers time to write *proposals*.

The weeks after the submission deadline are an exciting and very demanding time for the employees of the science agency that posted the solicitations, because they must sort the proposals into categories for the peer review. Strictly speaking, some of the scientists managing the new program are not government employees, because they are university faculty who have come on detail for a period of time, often two or three years, and will return to their universities when their tour of duty has finished. These *rotators* exemplify a different form of fluid democracy that might be applied more widely in government.

Let's say that 500 distinct proposals have been submitted. This is far too many to review in one lump, so they are divided into groups on the basis of the expertise required to evaluate them. After much reading and discussion, the program officers might divide them into 20 groups of 25, for example. Each of the 20 groups would be reviewed as a unit by one panel of reviewers, managed by one or two of the program officers. The managers of each panel then recruit reviewers, following some mixture of two different approaches.

It is possible to recruit separate reviewers for each proposal, what are called *ad-hoc reviewers*. It is also possible to recruit a group of *panelists*, each of whom would review several proposals. For example, a panel evaluating 25 proposals could have 10 panelists, each reviewing 10 proposals, to provide 4 reviews for each proposal. And of course, the panel could handle fully 50 proposals at this rate of review writing, if half the reviews were of the ad-hoc type. Each written review would have a summary rating of the quality of the proposal, plus text that might follow a template listing the criteria for the particular competition.

Great care is taken to avoid using reviewers who have a conflict of interest on the proposal, and typically nobody submitting to the particular competition can serve as a reviewer or panelist. The proposals and reviews are usually confidential, and everybody involved in the process swears to avoid exploiting any intellectual property that is in the proposals. Depending on the particular science agency, the panel may or may not precisely rank the proposals, but it certainly will separate those that deserve further consideration from those that do not. Again, depending on the rules of the particular agency, the program directors may have a significant role in deciding which of the fundable proposals to move forward for actual funding.

The entire process is Internet-facilitated. In addition to having computerized records of past reviews, the program officers have efficient tools for finding new reviewers, such as checking the rosters of recent conferences in the given area, and of course visiting academic websites. Reviewers and panelists are recruited via email. A special web-based information system handles the submission of proposals, and their distribution to the individuals who will be writing reviews. During a panel meeting, a well-designed groupware system gives panelists access to the proposals and reviews for their particular panel, allowing them to develop a collective written record of their deliberations, and to assign proposals to funding priority categories. A number of agencies have recently experimented with conducting the panel meeting itself online, using videoconferencing or even virtual worlds such as Second Life (Bohannon 2011).

We do not usually consider the rotators, reviewers, and panelists to be political representatives, because we tend to focus on their technical expertise rather than their values. Yet ideally they do represent the public through their judgment of how to achieve the goals that society seeks. I can imagine expanding this system - with whatever improvements we can devise - for decision-making outside science funding. Questionnaire surveys, recommender systems, and the form of fluid representation suggested by the Berlin committee could establish goals that the society wants to achieve. A fluid peer-review process could then work out the specific means to achieve them.

Devolution

In ancient times, political power was enforced by clubs and spears, and later emanated from the muzzle of a gun, so it was of necessity tied to a particular territory of land defended by an army. But if humanity can evolve beyond warfare, or at least be assured of peace within wide territorial units, then the ultimate basis of the state need no longer be military in nature. That means that government actions and policies may be developed and applied in a manner more subtle than territorial defense. With the Internet, political constituencies need no longer be defined in terms of geographic districts, but can devolve to the subgroups of humanity most concerned with any issue. Thus it becomes possible to achieve what Bruce Tonn and David Feldman (1995) called *non-spatial government*.

There have been examples in the past when governmental jurisdictions overlapped to some degree, depending upon different functions that were performed. Voting districts, school districts, and postal delivery areas often fail to coincide. The Tennessee Valley Authority was created by the United States government in 1933 to serve energy needs and manage resources in an area covering portions of seven states. President Roosevelt conceptualized it as a new kind of organization, "a corporation clothed with the power of government but possessed of the flexibility and initiative of a private enterprise" [URL 8]. However one may judge that particular experiment, which continues to the present day, it suggests that for certain purposes even old-fashioned forms of government could aggregate geographic areas in different ways for different purposes.

Today's communication technology allows us to escape geographic boundaries altogether, for some public purposes. Just as fluid democracy seeks to assemble people into networks in which temporary opinion leaders may represent constantly fluctuating constituencies, the scope of decision-making and policy application may be geographically different for every topic, and at each historical moment. For some policy issues, quite different systems may coexist in a given area, but serving different constituencies.

A good hypothetical example is marriage laws. In secular societies, marriage is no longer a sacred institution bound by traditional customs, but a kind of contract, and there can be many different versions. Over the course of human history, a wide range of marital practices abounded. Whatever we may personally think of them, many ancient societies had strict rules of exogamy, forbidding marriage within culturally defined segments of society (Levi-Strauss 1969), others permitted polygamy, and others differed greatly in the rules governing erotic behavior among young people (Malinowsky 1927). Why should decisions about the legitimacy of different practices be decided by the particular latitude and longitude where the people live?

Given the liberalization of local laws relating to marriage, one could imagine multiple worldwide networks arising, each representing people who wished to follow a particular marital system. In most cases, the network would be of only modest importance in a family's life, and for other purposes its members would be embedded in quite different networks, including one representing their geographic neighbors. The marriage network would develop the precise standards for the particular kind of marriage contract, might have as a minor adjunct an online dating service, and offer marital counseling and courts appropriate for its particular principles. It would judge cases of marital discord - except the most violent outbursts which might need to be handled locally - and define the remedies for most problems. Only people who had married within the system of a given network would participate in its political processes, but they could live anywhere on the planet.

It is possible that over time many institutions of society would become non-spatial, or at least allowing several alternative, specialized political networks to occupy the same territory. In major cities, there already exist multiple schools systems - secular, religious, public, private, charter - as well as home schooling in the United States for many families. Laws would need to be changed to permit public funding of religious schools, but each system could be funded only by its own constituency, so that nobody was required to pay taxes for a kind of education with which they did not approve. Multiple overlapping school systems would therefore have their own fluid democracy political systems, each designed to satisfy the particular needs of its constituency.

Whether we are really prepared to move toward non-spatial government, the worldwide digital communication network permits it. Marriages and schools may not even be the best examples of institutions ready to evolve beyond the limitations of local geography. Internet provides the world great freedom, along many dimensions of human action and experience, and we will need wisdom greater than any individual can possess, to know which directions to explore first.

Intellectual Property

The idea that government should regulate intellectual property through copyrights and patents is relatively recent in human history, and the precise details of what intellectual property is protected for how long vary across nations and occasionally change (Bainbridge 2003). As a scientist, I am offended by the fact that scientists are accorded no legal rights with respect to their discoveries, which may have required intellectual genius and exhausting labor to achieve, whereas an engineer who tinkers up a new device can often patent it, and even rotten authors can copyright their scribblings. There are two standard sociological justifications for patents or copyrights: They reward creators for their labor, and they encourage greater creativity. Both of these are empirical claims that can be tested scientifically and could be false in some realms (Ganz-Brown 1998; National Research Council 2000).

Consider music (Bainbridge 2000). Star performers existed before the 20th century, such as Franz Liszt and Niccolo Paganini, but mass media produced a celebrity system promoting a few stars whose music was not necessarily the best or most diverse. Copyright provides protection for distribution companies and for a few celebrities, thereby helping to support the industry as currently defined, but it may actually harm the majority of performers. This is comparable to Anatole France's famous irony, "The law, in its majestic equality, forbids the rich as well as the poor to sleep under bridges." In theory, copyright covers the creations of celebrities and obscurities equally, but only major distribution companies have the resources to defend their property rights in court. In a sense, this is quite fair, because nobody wants to steal unpopular music, but by supporting the property rights of celebrities, copyright strengthens them as a class in contrast to anonymous musicians.

Government deregulation of music - ending copyright - could reduce the advantage of centralized music production over decentralized and diverse music. In a deregulated market, the Internet could help myriads of local and noncommercial musicians find audiences. Arguably, the communication technologies of the twentieth century commercialized culture, but now the Internet may decommercialize it by eroding the power of the distribution corporations.

Internet music file sharing has become a significant factor in the social lives of children, who download bootleg music tracks for their own use and to give as gifts to friends. Thus, on the level of families, ending copyright could be morally as well as economically advantageous. On a much higher level, however, the culture-exporting nations (notably the United States) could stand to lose, although we cannot really predict the net balance of costs and benefits in the absence of proper research. We do not presently have good cross-national data on file sharing or a well-developed theoretical framework to guide research on whether copyright protection supports cultural imperialism versus enhancing the positions of diverse cultures in the global marketplace.

It will not be easy to test such hypotheses, and extensive economic research has not conclusively answered the question of whether the patent system really promotes innovation. We will need many careful, sharp-focus studies of well-formed hypotheses in specific industries and sectors of life. For example, observational and interview research can uncover the factors that really promote cultural innovation among artists of various kinds and determine the actual consequences for children of Internet peer-to-peer file sharing. However, there seems to be little interest on the part of government research-funding agencies to look at politically sensitive issues like this, so while science will be a central part of our future revolution, it is not in a position to fire the first shots.

Quite apart from the economics of music, there are also many questions in the space between governance of creativity and music technology. A half century ago, a very different technology existed that had political implications, namely tape recorders, which I can describe from first-hand knowledge. I obtained my first tape recorder in 1958. This was actually two years *later* than I obtained my first computer game, the remarkable Geniac.

For several years, I used tape recorders to make personal copies of classical music from New York City FM radio stations, including many European avant-garde concerts that never appeared on commercial recordings. It never occurred to me I was violating anybody's intellectual property rights. My third and fourth tape recorders were quarter-track stereo machines that could put two hours of high-fidelity monophonic music on a single cheap tape. The radio stations published their schedules well in advance, so it was both fun and easy to make these recordings. There was little incentive to make copies for friends, both because they had different musical tastes, and because copying was more tedious than the original recording, requiring two machines plus a fair amount of labor, and added noise to the recording. Today's DVDs and online file sharing make copying easier, but also there has been a shift in who copies what kind of music for what purpose. Reel-to-reel tape recorders like the ones I had half a century ago were often used to record live events, and were not a good technology with which to deliver popular music to the masses.

There is the real political dimension in this issue. Music distribution companies, and the mass media in general, exploit people through advertising that uses many tricks to get them to buy culturally inferior products. Teenage children, physically exhausted working class families, and people who are socially isolated from the local musical culture, learn to gobble up the latest recordings by celebrities. In general, we should seek the decommercialization of the arts, even as we seek new ways to reward very large numbers of artists in their local communities.

This brings us back to devolution, and to new technology-based forms of democracy. On the one hand, we can simply abolish copyrights and watch the music distribution industry wither away, as already seems to be happening with respect to magazines and newspapers. Or, we could create such attractive free sources of music, that the masses liberated themselves from their current cultural thralldom, and simply stopped buying recorded music, but gave the money instead to their local singer-songwriter. More likely, several things will happen at once, and a variety of collective decisions will need to be made by governments, guilds of performers, and segments of the general public. The online devolved decision-processes described above will then come in handy for music and the many subcultures within it, as it will for the art arts and many other dimensions of life.

Conclusion

Fluid democracy can be considered a high-tech approach for improving existing government institutions, or it can be considered a revolutionary approach that would entirely replace them. Indeed, one of the adjustment mechanisms that can be built into the new system could be how revolutionary it is in practice. For example, if fluid democracy completely replaces the old system, then all of the financial obligations incurred under the old system become void. If investors see fluid democracy rising in political significance, they would be well advised to sell any government bonds they hold, because these "securities" very well could become worthless if the new system in fact took power. Once fluid democracy was in place, the new system could avoid government debt by allocating funding across government departments in terms of a percentage of tax revenues, rather than as defined dollar amounts. That allocation could be decided annually as voters told the government database what fraction of their own taxes they wanted to go to each department, or which political party they wanted to make that decision for them.

Clearly, we have a long road to travel before fluid democracy can be a reality. In addition to political activism, much research and technology development will be required. A large number of pieces must be assembled to complete the puzzle. Yet it is clear that traditional political structures are failing, so the opportunity for healthy but radical change has now arrived, with the maturity of Internet, at this particular point in human history.

PRIVATIZING LIFE
KEMBREW MCLEOD

Because of a landmark Supreme Court case and congressional legislation, 1980 was a pivotal year for genetic research. In the *Diamond v. Chakrabarty* decision, a five-to-four majority ruled that a living, genetically altered microorganism could be patented under U.S. law. Previous to this ruling, it was the policy of the U.S. Patent and Trademark Office (PTO) that living organisms— in the case of *Diamond v. Chakrabarty,* a bacterium that helped clean oil spills— could not be patented. But the Supreme Court ruled otherwise, stating that "anything under the sun that is made by the hand of man" is patentable subject matter. That same year, Congress passed the Bayh-Dole Act to encourage the commercialization of inventions produced by universities and other recipients of federal funding. An influx of private money poured into university science departments, and since the act's passing, the private funding of university biomedical research has increased by a factor of 20.

This growth in subsidies provided the legal justification for researchers to exploit human genes. And when I use the word "exploit," I'm not using it in an ideological way— I'm simply using the terminology of a patent lawyer. During an interview with a *New York Times* reporter,

Todd Dickinson, the former U.S. Patent and Trademark Office's commissioner, took exception to the idea that patents allow a "government sponsored monopoly," a phrase he found imprecise. Instead, Commissioner Dickinson corrected the reporter, saying candidly and without irony, "We like to say 'right to exploit.' "Today, private pharmaceutical companies (many of which are partnered with universities) are engaged in a manic— maniacal, even— race to patent every imaginable human gene, protein, and cell line that might be profitable.

The BRCA-1 and BRCA-2 genes are linked to breast cancer and are owned by Myriad Genetics, whose literature reports, "Women with a BRCA mutation have a 33 to 50 percent risk of developing cancer by age 50 and a 56 to 87 percent risk by age 70."Myriad has a monopoly right over the use of the gene in diagnostic tests or therapies, which means that every time a woman is tested to find out if she carries those mutated genes, a hefty royalty has to be paid to Myriad. Also, if a researcher discovers a therapy that prevents cancerous mutations in these genes, he or she is obligated under the law to secure a license from Myriad, and the company has used its patent to block research on the gene. This is one of the ways that these kinds of gene patents contribute to the skyrocketing costs of drugs and medical care in the United States and throughout the world.

Helena Chaye, like many I've spoken with in the business of drugs and science, feels uncomfortable about these kinds of situations. As the director of Business Development at the biotech corporation MediGene, she secures and sells gene patent licenses for the company. Chaye finds herself in an uneasy position. She has both a Ph.D. in molecular genetics and a degree in law, and is intimately familiar with both areas. "From a private company's perspective," she tells me, "you want everything to be protected. You want the ability to block other people, and you want the ability to monopolize a certain sector or a certain product and block others from entering, even though you may not be the one [who's] actually developing it." For many commercial entities, it simply makes no business sense to put anything in the public domain.

"I personally don't believe in that," Chaye says. "From what I do for a living, it's a struggle, philosophically, that I'm having to patent everything." She continues: "If genetic sequencing was publicly available for diagnostics, for example, you wouldn't have to go through Myriad and pay four thousand dollars for a breast cancer test. If that was available to other parties, then you could have somebody else develop it at a much cheaper rate and be available for everyone." She pauses. "I mean, the flip side of that is they say, 'Well, we're not going to be able to develop something so expensive unless there's some sort of monopoly that protects us in the future.' But I think there's a reasonable level at which certain things should be protected, and certain things should be left to the public domain."

My favorite patent request was submitted by a British waitress and poet who protested the gobbling up of the genetic commons by filing patent application GB0000180.0. She wanted to patent herself.

"It has taken 30 years of hard labor for me to discover and invent myself," Donna MacLean drily wrote in the application, "and now I wish to protect my invention from unauthorized exploitation, genetic or otherwise. I am new. I have led a private existence and I have not made the invention of myself public." MacLean added, "I am not obvious." The provocateur poet didn't receive her patent, but she made her point.

PATENTS AS STUMBLING BLOCKS

While many are still happily riding the moneymaking bandwagon, there are a growing number of scientists, medical researchers, and even companies that believe certain gene patents can inhibit research. The chief scientific officer at Bristol-Myers Squibb, Peter Ringrose— hardly a radical anti-capitalist Luddite— said that there were "more than fifty proteins possibly involved in cancer that the company was not working on because the patent holders either would not allow it or were demanding unreasonable royalties." Dr. Gareth Evans, a consultant in medical genetics, also believes that the economic value of genetic patents make research more secretive and restrictive, and therefore lessens the chances of scientists finding cures.

The hoarding of these kinds of patents threatens to create a "tragedy of the anti-commons," as Rebecca Eisenberg, a National Institutes of Heath-affiliated law professor at the University of Michigan, calls it. The phrase "tragedy of the commons" was coined by Garrett Hardin in his classic essay of the same name, and its primary argument goes like this: If anyone can use common property— a pasture where farm animals can freely graze, for instance— then it can be overused and trashed. While this can happen to physical resources, a patented gene won't suffer the same fate, but as Eisenberg points out by inverting the phrase, tragedies *do* occur from fencing off the genetic commons. Yes, it's true that patent protection provides the financial incentive for companies to invest in research and development, which, in turn, generates many useful drugs and inventions. Patents aren't inherently bad, but Eisenberg argues that certain patents can be problematic when the protected materials resemble a discovery, rather than an invention.

This kind of patent ownership creates bureaucratic stumbling blocks and economic disincentives that can dissuade laboratories from dealing with certain genes. This was the case with hemochromatosis, a hereditary condition that can cause liver or heart failure (the gene that carries the disorder is found in one in ten people). In 1999 two companies were fighting over the ownership rights of the patented gene connected to hemochromatosis. This created confusion over who owned the patent and to whom medical laboratories should pay licensing fees, helping to shut down research on DNA tests that screened for the condition. Five labs halted testing for hemochromatosis, and twenty-one others decided not to offer the test at all.[1]

Professor Eisenberg argues that the existence of a genetic commons speeds efficiency in medical research because it eliminates the need to track down and negotiate with numerous patent owners.

This point was highlighted in 1999 when ten of the world's largest drug companies created an alliance with five of the leading gene laboratories. The alliance invested in a two-year plan to uncover and publish three hundred thousand common genetic variations to prevent upstart biotechnology companies from patenting and locking up important genetic information. The companies (including Bayer AG and Bristol-Myers Squibb) wanted the data released into the public domain to ensure that genetic information could be freely accessed and used for research. Its mission undermined the assertion that a genetic commons inevitably leads to commercial suicide and the end of research incentives.[2]

What's most troubling about thousands of DNA sequences being owned by a handful of companies is the fact that genes are deeply interrelated. For instance, there is no single gene that causes Alzheimer's disease, which instead results from a variety of environ-mental factors and interactions with other genes. Scientists have mapped much of the human genome, figuring out that there are roughly one hundred thousand pieces of a genetic jigsaw puzzle. But in order to effectively fight diseases with genetic technologies, researchers have to learn how each privately owned gene connects and reacts with the ones around it. Imagine trying to put together a puzzle if you had to buy a random assortment of jigsaw pieces from dozens of companies. You might get frustrated, even give up. When you have to secure multiple licenses from several companies just to begin research, it is all the more difficult for scientists to efficiently and affordably do their job.

No Safe Harbor

"It's a really big problem if you have to sign lots of agreements," Eisenberg told *New Scientist.* "Licenses and material transfer agreements with companies are taking longer to negotiate, so it may take weeks or months." Similarly, Jeffrey Kahn, director of the University of Minnesota's Center for Bioethics, cautioned that high licensing fees can hold medical progress hostage. "If you're a start-up company, you need to have those licenses bagged," MediGene's Helena Chaye tells me. "You need them in your back pocket to go and raise money or to entice investors to put more money into it because you've got new licensed technologies." Not having those licenses, she says, "could definitely hinder your operations."And if you think that many of these companies aren't aggressively guarding their genes, just listen to Human Genome Sciences CEO William A. Haseltine, who openly stated: "Any company that wants to be in the business of using genes, proteins or antibodies as drugs has a very high probability of running afoul of our patents. From a commercial point of view, they are severely constrained— and far more than they realize."

Geneticist John Sulston argues in his book, *The Common Thread* that it seems unlikely "that patent laws combined with untrammeled market forces are going to lead to a resolution that is in the best interests of further research, or of human health and well being." Advocates of privatization argue that having a commons that anyone can freely draw from will mean the end of creativity and innovation, but the opposite is often true. The way patent law is applied in genetics can limit researchers' choices, which means the scientific imagination becomes routinized and stifled. There's little room for the kinds of visionary ideas and accidental discoveries that evolve into real breakthroughs. An argument for the commons— whether it's the genetic commons or a folk-song commons— is an argument for more creative elbow room. [3] But because of our blind faith in privatization, freedom of expression® has been limited artistically, socially, and scientifically.

SEEDS = INFORMATION

I live in Iowa, and I am surrounded by corn, pork, pickup trucks, and, from what I hear, meth labs. Over the past few years, I've been inundated by plenty of weird and wonderful stories about farming and rural living. However, one of the most unsettling, science fiction–sounding scenarios I've come across is the "Technology Protection System," or "terminator technology," as it is known in the press. This technology enables seed companies to genetically alter their patented seeds so that crops become sterile after one planting, turning off life like a light switch. It's a way of preventing farmers from retaining seeds from the previous year's crop and replanting them.

Saving and replanting seeds is something we humans have been doing since we stopped being nomadic creatures, but the practice is now illegal with seeds that are patented. The terminator seeds were developed by the U.S.–based Delta and Pine Land, whose president trumpeted, "We expect the new technology to have global implications."Delta and Pine Land claimed that the terminator seed would be marketed primarily in developing countries to prevent farmers from saving, trading, and/or replanting seeds that are sold by U.S. corporations. Interestingly, the seed industry experienced many aspects of the Napster file-sharing controversy a few years before it hit the music industry.

While there are obvious differences, there are also striking similarities. MP3 music files circulate on the Internet because someone had to purchase a CD, which was then inserted into a computer and "ripped" into digital files. These files can then be exactly duplicated, and copies are made of these copies, then shared. This is also true of privately owned seeds, though the earth (rather than a computer) "reaps" this information without permission. These copied seeds can then be given to other farmers through informal trading systems, delivering them from person to person, a sort of rural peer-to-peer file-sharing network. Even though the seeds are patented, much like music is copyrighted, this can't stop someone from creating a facsimile of someone else's intellectual property. This is why the terminator technology was invented.

Sterile seeds may be an inconvenience for American farmers who, for various reasons— including being riddled with debt— want to continue saving seeds. But they may prove devastating for their poorer counterparts in Third World countries who rely on subsistence farming. U.S. Department of Agriculture (USDA) spokesperson Willard Phelps stated that the goal of the terminator technology is "to increase the value of proprietary seed owned by U.S. seed companies and to open new markets in second and Third World countries." The primary creator of the terminator seed, Melvin J. Oliver, made clear his invention's purpose to *New Scientist:* "Our system is a way of self-policing the unauthorized use of American technology," he asserted, comparing it to copy-protection technologies that prevent the duplication of music. And we wonder why so much of the world hates us.

In mid-1998 Monsanto made an attempt to purchase terminator seed– patent owner Delta and Pine Land. However, this technology met with heated worldwide protests that targeted Monsanto as the next Great Satan, and in early 1999 the company stepped back in "recognition that we need some level of public acceptance to do our business." Although Monsanto backed out of the merger, Delta and Pine Land, which still holds the terminator-seed patent with the USDA, has continued to develop the technology. Just as in the movies, the Terminator lived on. Delta and Pine Land official Harry Collins stated in January 2000, "We've continued right on with work on the Technology Protection System. We never really slowed down. We're on target,moving ahead to commercialize it. We never really backed off." Since then, more terminator-technology patents have been awarded.

Four-fifths of the sixteen hundred patents issued for genetically modified crops are owned by just thirteen companies, and some of the most significant patents belong to Monsanto. The St. Louis–based operation was founded in 1901 as a chemical company, and it gained notoriety in the 1970s because it was responsible for creating Agent Orange. This chemical compound was used by the military to clear jungles in Vietnam, which led to illness and death in thousands, and the company has also been implicated in several cases of employee and residential contamination. A Monsanto production plant contaminated the Missouri town of Times Beach so much that it had to be evacuated in 1982, and in 2002 Monsanto lost a case against lawyers representing a small Alabama town that had been poisoned as well.[4]

By the mid-1990s Monsanto moved much of its chemical operations to biotechnology, and it is now a global leader in transgenic crops. The contract for Monsanto's Roundup Ready soybeans allows the company to search a customer's farmland for signs of saved seeds, and, to nab offenders, the company can track purchase records and check with seed dealers. Among other things, the company has hired Pinkerton detectives— the same private police force hired by the Rockefellers to murderously bust unions in the 1920s— to investigate tips on seed saving. In addition, the company created and advertised the existence of hotlines for neighbors to report farmers who save seeds. "Dial 1–800–ROUNDUP," said a Monsanto ad. "Tell the rep that you want to report some potential seed law violations or other information. It is important to use 'land lines' rather than cellular phones due to the number of people who scan cellular calls."[5]

Monsanto also developed a kit that determines whether or not a plant was derived from patented seeds by using a principle similar to a pregnancy test, but applied to leaves. Scott Good was one of the many farmers who dealt with the wrath of Monsanto when he saved his seeds and replanted the company's intellectual property. "They showed up at my door at six o'clock in the morning. They flipped a badge," said Scott of Monsanto's agents. "They acted like the FBI. I was scared." Farmers who infringe on Monsanto's patents have been fined hundreds of thousands of dollars, and some face bankruptcy. Much like other large seed companies, Monsanto offers incentives for seed distributors to carry their patented seeds rather than public-domain seeds.

A farmer's choice to plant public-domain seeds becomes increasingly difficult or impossible when near-monopolies exist within the agribusiness industries. Factory farming has flooded the market with low-priced crops, which forces farmers to purchase the patented, high-yield seeds or go out of business. University of Indiana seed geneticist Martha Crouch commented to *Science* magazine, "Free choice is a nice idea, but it doesn't seem to operate in the real world." Although critics have blasted the existence of these so-called Frankenfoods, we should keep in mind that farmers throughout history have manipulated the genetic makeup of crops by selecting for certain favorable traits. Also, these genetically modified crops often grow in more abundant quantities, need less labor, and sometimes require fewer chemical pesticides or herbicides. In other words, there are reasons why North American farmers plant these seeds.

One of the trade-offs, however, is that these patented crops are also uniform in their genetic makeup. This is a problem because when we rely on fewer varieties of food, we increase our chances of exposing ourselves to major food shortages. For instance, the biological cause of the Irish Potato Famine in the mid-1800s was rooted in a reliance on two major varieties of potatoes. The *Phytophthorainfestans* fungus precipitated the destruction of Ireland's primary food staple for five years, spreading to the Highlands of Scotland and elsewhere. Although the same blight affected the Andes, because South American farmers preserved hundreds of varieties of potatoes, the effects of the fungus were minimal. In fact, the only reason the Europeans could restock their food supply was that they could draw on varieties of potatoes from the Andean region.[6]

The spread of uniform, patented seeds has accelerated the loss of thousands of varieties of crops. Today, 97 percent of the vegetable varieties sold by commercial seed houses in the United States at the beginning of the century are now extinct, and 86 percent of the fruit varieties have been lost. These numbers are actually quite conservative because there were surely more varieties that weren't collected in the nineteenth century. Over the twentieth century the varieties of cabbage dropped from 544 to 20; carrots from 287 to 21; cauliflower from 158 to 9; apples from 7,089 to 878. The list goes on. In sum, roughly 75 percent of the genetic diversity of the world's twenty most important food crops has been lost *forever*. Because biodiversity is a key factor in the ability of plants to adapt to changing conditions, and humans' ability to do the same, reduced biodiversity seriously threatens ecological support systems.[7]

Despite skepticism from Europe, the planting of altered (and patented) soybeans, corn, potatoes, and canola in the United States and Canada has exploded, and the market for such crops is expected to grow to as much as $500 billion in the next few decades. The dramatic rise in the growing of patented crops in North America will likely be followed by the same expansion in other countries throughout the world— one way or the other. It's a biological fact that, once the pollen from genetically modified crops travels through the air, it can pollinate nongenetically modified crops. This invasive pollination has happened to many organic farmers, such as Laura Krouse, based in Iowa. Because of the presence of the Bt gene in her corn, Krouse's crop can no longer be certified as organic, and she lost half her business in the process.

Why can't these farmers prevent this contamination? The answer, my friend, is blowing in the wind. "I don't know if there's room for a business like mine anymore," said Krouse. "Biologically, it doesn't seem like it's going to be possible because of this sea of genetically engineered pollen that I live in, over which I have no control."[8] In

1998 Monsanto sued Canadian farmer Percy Schmeiser after the company discovered its patented canola plants growing on his property. The seventy-three-year-old Schmeiser argued that he shouldn't have to pay Monsanto a licensing fee because the pollen had blown onto his property from neighboring farms. Although Monsanto said this might be the case— in fact, the company acknowledged that Schmeiser never placed an order for its Roundup Ready canola— he was still infringing on their patent.

In a narrow 5–4 decision, Canada's Supreme Court ruled in favor of Monsanto in 2004, stating that it wasn't concerned with "blow by" dissemination of patented plants. It simply determined that the farmer "actively cultivated" Monsanto's property. These patented seeds have also traveled south because the North American Free Trade Agreement (NAFTA) allows five million tons of corn to be sold in Mexico. Many residents of the country, and the Mexican government itself, are up in arms over what they see as an unwelcome invasion of their farmlands. But Dr. Michael Phillips, an executive director at the Biotechnology Industry Organization (BIO), isn't very sympathetic. "If you're the government of Mexico, hopefully you've learned a lesson here," he bluntly told *NOW with Bill Moyers.* The lesson? "It's very difficult to keep a new technology from, you know, entering your borders— particularly in a biological system."

GLOBALIZATION AND ITS DISCONTENTS

Much of the developing world— primarily rain-forest countries— is loaded with what some gene hunters refer to as "green gold." This refers to medically useful plant materials that can yield massive profits. However, identifying a valuable DNA sequence is a very difficult task, like finding a needle in a mountainous biological haystack. Scientists working for Western companies get around this problem by relying on tribal shamans and medicine men to point them to plants that are medically useful. Using the knowledge developed by indigenous people in developing countries increases by 400-fold a scientist's ability to locate the plants that have specific medicinal uses. In another estimate, by consulting with the local communities, bioprospectors can increase the success ratio from one in ten thousand samples to one in two in their quest to find active ingredients that can be used in medicines.

For instance, using an active ingredient extracted from an indigenous plant in northeastern Brazil, the U.S.–based MGI Pharma developed a drug to treat symptoms of xerostomia, or "dry-mouth syndrome." The drug's development capitalized on the local knowledge about the properties of the jaborandi plant, which literally means— I love this —"slobber-mouth plant." Knowledge about the plant's properties had been passed down for generations, but the company did not compensate the native Brazilians in any way. Nor did MGI Pharma have to, even though it was the local knowledge that led the U.S. researchers to the drug discovery in the first place.[9]

Over the centuries, indigenous communities have significantly contributed to the diversity and cultivation of our most basic and important crops. The reason why we can purchase blue corn tortilla chips in stores is because of the centuries of care Mexican farmers gave to cultivating varieties of blue corn (as well as yellow, white, red, speckled, and hundreds of other varieties). This cultivation is a form of labor; that this corn still exists is no mere accident. However, only the knowledge developed in scientific laboratories is protected as patented "property,"while the traditional systems are open to plundering because they are communally maintained. This illustrates the double-edged nature of "the commons," a reason why this concept shouldn't be blindly celebrated in all situations.

Under the global patent system, intellectual property can only be produced by people in white lab coats employed by companies with huge amounts of capital at their disposal. The time and labor and collective achievements of indigenous farmers are rendered worthless, devalued as being merely "nature." These kinds of bioprospecting patents— or, as globalization critic Vandana Shiva calls them, *biopiracy patents*— are built on the fiction of individualistic scientific innovation. This false premise ignores the collective nature of knowledge and denies communities patent protection.[10]

It would be as if someone came along and copyrighted the stories in the Bible. The Old Testament's narratives were passed down from generation to generation through the oral tradition, preserved by hundreds and thousands of years of active storytelling. Those who set the stories into print certainly had a strong editorial hand, crafting the sentences and ordering the stories in unique ways. But there are still strong echoes of that oral tradition: the use of repetition, mnemonics, formula, and other devices common to oral folk narratives. The written version of the Old Testament simply could not exist without the effort of the communities who passed the stories on. The same is true of useful plants in Third World countries.

Western scientists would have never "discovered" these plants if not for the cultivative labor of indigenous communities over hundreds and thousands of years. Unfortunately, this is not an argument that makes sense in most established theories of economics— so, to paraphrase Woody Guthrie, the poor people lose again. The U.N.'s 1999 *Human Development Report* pointed out that more than half of the most frequently prescribed drugs throughout the world have been derived from plants, plant genes, or plant extracts from developing countries. These drugs are a standard part of the treatment of lymphatic cancer, glaucoma, leukemia, and various heart conditions, and they account for billions in annual sales.

According to the United Nations Development Project study, developing countries annually lose $5 billion in unpaid royalties from drugs developed from medicinal plants. The United States sees it differently. It calculates that developing countries owe its pharmaceutical companies $2.5 billion for violating their medical patents.[11]

The case of the yellow Mexican bean patent is symbolic of how patents can enable economic colonialism, where resources are drained from developing countries. In the early 1990s, bioprospector Larry Proctor bought a bag of dry beans in Mexico and proceeded to remove the yellow varieties, allowing them to pollinate.

After he had a "uniform and stable population" of yellow beans, his company, POD-NERS, exercised its legal right of monopoly by suing two companies that imported the yellow Mexican beans. The president of Tutuli Produce, Rebecca Gilliland, stated: "In the beginning, I thought it was a joke. How could [Proctor] invent something that Mexicans have been growing for centuries?" POD-NERS demanded a royalty of six cents per pound on the import of these yellow beans, which prompted U.S. customs officials to inspect shipments and take samples of Mexican beans at the border, at an additional cost to Gilliland's company.

Her company lost customers, as did other companies, which meant that twenty-two thousand Mexican farmers lost 90 percent of their income. The Mexican government challenged the U.S. patent on this bean variety, but the process would be long and costly, running at least two hundred thousand dollars in legal fees. In the meantime, Proctor remained defiant, filing lawsuits against sixteen small bean-seed companies and farmers in Colorado, and he amended the original patent with forty-three new claims. Poorer countries typically don't have the resources to battle these types of patents, especially when there are more pressing domestic concerns such as clean-water availability and health emergencies.[12] This lack of means to challenge bioprospectors is a real concern for countries targeted by patent-happy multinationals. It's a problem because the economies of some African countries rely on only one export, and others, on only four or five.

These exports are essentially raw biological materials, and they make up roughly 40 percent of all the world's processing and production. But once corporate biotechnology reduces active ingredients found in developing countries to their molecular components, the commodity can be manufactured rather than grown. Western multinationals hold a vast amount of patents on naturally occur-ring biological materials found in the Southern Hemisphere. These companies own 79 percent of all utility patents on plants; Northern universities and research institutions control 14 percent; and parties in Third World countries have almost no holdings. In Mexico, for example, in 1996 only 389 patent applications came from Mexican residents, while over 30,000 came from foreign residents. In this way, intellectual-property laws help to exacerbate the unequal distribution of wealth among rich and poor nations.[13]

Although patent law carries with it a Western bias, that doesn't mean the future is a bleak, foregone conclusion for developing countries. In recent years, these nations and their allies within nongovernmental organizations have lobbied strongly to better protect the resources of countries rich in traditional knowledge and biodiversity. For instance, the World Intellectual Property Organization (WIPO) convened the "Intergovernmental Committee on Intellectual Property and Genetic Resources, Traditional Knowledge, and Folklore"—which met seven times between 2000 and 2004. The committee's goal is manifold, but with regard to genetic resources it aims to encourage "benefit sharing" agreements between companies and countries rich in valuable biological material.[14]

An example of this is a 1991 deal linked between the pharmaceutical company Merck and the Costa Rican nonprofit Instituto Nacional de Biodiversidad (INBio). The agreement held the potential for Costa Rica to earn more than $100 million annually, money generated from INBio's 10,000 collected samples of biological material. Although INBio signed more than ten similar contracts with other companies, it should be noted that these kinds of agreements are entirely voluntary and continue to be rare. In fact, Merck ended its association with INBio in 1999, and no royalties had been earned as of 2004. Lorena

Guevara, the manager of bioprospecting at INBio, told me that negotiations with companies over the terms of benefit sharing are quite difficult. Still, Guevara remains optimistic,even in the face of forces that are much more powerful than the nonprofit for which she works — or, for that matter, Costa Rica itself.

North American and European countries, and particularly the United States, have led an unrelenting battle to force developing countries to adopt acceptable (to them) intellectual-property systems.

The Trade-Related Aspects of Intellectual Property Rights (TRIPS) has been an instrumental tool that forces member countries of the World Trade Organization (WTO) to adopt standardized intellectual-property laws. The general public in the First and Third World had no say in writing TRIPS. A senior U.S. trade negotiator remarked that, "probably less than fifty people were responsible for TRIPS."[15] TRIPS forces developing countries to adopt intellectual-property laws that often run counter to their national interests, and if they don't comply, they're threatened with economic blackmail in the form of trade retaliations.

Strengthened intellectual-property laws in developing countries decreases the ability of local communities to gain access to technological information (through reverse engineering and other imitative methods). This makes technological catching-up all the more difficult. In this brave new privatized world, the only way to have market power is to innovate. But the only way to innovate is to have lots of capital to invest in the first place, and developing countries only account for 6 percent of global research and development expenditures. As poor nations strengthen their intellectual-property regimes, their markets increasingly are dominated by imported goods, because their local industries can't compete.

The WTO acts as a policing mechanism that allows countries to bring "unfair competition" charges and other actions against offending countries. For instance, the Bush 2.0 administration has been under pressure from the biotech industry to bring charges against the European Union for its ban against genetically modified food. In a letter to Bush signed by virtually every agribusiness and biotech firm, it claimed that the ban stigmatized biotechnology and "may be negatively affecting the attitudes and actions of other countries." As if other countries should not dare form their own opinions and policies.

For years, the United States opposed in WTO courts the waiving of patents in countries that have been overwhelmed by AIDS and other deadly diseases, making it illegal for those countries to import generic versions of drugs at a fraction of the cost. Economic studies of Taiwan, China, and India have shown that when patent laws are strengthened, drug prices go up because these countries can no longer manufacture generic drugs. This pattern has been repeated numerous times in poorer countries, where price increases can be devastating. During the 1990s, the Brazilian government was proactive in dealing with AIDS, allowing local pharmaceutical manufacturers to produce low-cost generic HIV therapies. It wrote its patent laws to allow for what's called compulsory licensing, which legally compels owners to license their patents at a rate regulated by the government.

This approach allowed Brazilian manufacturers to produce Nevirapine — which helps prevent mother-to-child HIV transmission— for an affordable amount. It cost $0.59 U.S. dollars a day to treat each victim, which resulted in a 50 percent drop in AIDS related mortality between 1996 and 1999. As a reward for this achievement, the United States took Brazil to the WTO dispute panel to force the country to undo its liberal patent laws.[16] "The power of the rich countries and of the transnational corporations," argued John Sulston, "was being used in a bullying and inequitable fashion to achieve ends that benefit them rather than mankind as a whole." After years of worldwide pressure, the United States granted concessions in the WTO that were largely meaningless, like a provision that allowed countries to manufacture lifesaving drugs with-out penalty. However, most of these African countries had no such pharmaceutical production base, making it impossible for them to legally acquire the drugs.

Years dragged on, millions upon millions died until, in 2001, the United States agreed on a proposal that allows countries to import manufactured generic drugs. But under pressure from the pharmaceutical industry, the Bush 2.0 administration quietly changed its position and sent its trade representative to the WTO to kill the proposal. Much of the world reacted with rage to this shift, and finally in 2003 the United States signed on to an agreement that technically allowed countries with no manufacturing base to import cheap lifesaving drugs. I use the word "technically" because the agreement contains so much red tape that it severely limits the amount of supplies it can import. "Today's deal was designed to offer comfort to the U.S. and the Western pharmaceutical industry," said Ellen Hoen of the medical-aid group Doctors Without Borders. She told the Associated Press, "Unfortunately it offers little comfort for poor patients. Global patent rules will continue to drive up the price of medicines."

I only hope that she is wrong, though given the WTO's and the pharmaceutical industry's track record on this issue, I have little faith. The kinds of constraints intellectual-property laws impose on culture may be bad for music and creativity, but in the case of drug patents it's literally a life-and-death matter. Patent policy is as much a moral issue as it is an economic one, solid proof that property rights trump human rights nine times out of ten. Yes, I realize that these pharmaceutical companies invest millions of dollars in research and development, but there are times when profits alone shouldn't guide us and empathy and compassion should take over. However, we're living in a time when, increasingly, money is the only thing that matters.

I'm not claiming that all patents are bad things, because it's demonstrable that they can encourage investment in the development of products. However, I am arguing for two things. First, there should be some flexibility in the way patent protections are enforced, especially in situations such as the worldwide AIDS crisis. It simply should not have taken ten years for the WTO to adopt halfhearted rules about importing generic drugs, and I believe that those who tried to block it have blood on their hands. Second, there are too many instances when overly broad patents are awarded, which can cause information flow to be slowed and research and innovation to be stunted.

ONE FINAL IRONY

The most shameful detail in all of this is that all developing countries— whether they were the United States and Switzerland in the nineteenth century or Brazil and Thailand in the twentieth century— had very weak patent and copyright laws. Historically, countries left out of the technological-development loop have emphasized the right of their citizens to have free access to foreign inventions and knowledge. The United States in particular had extremely lax intellectual-property laws at the turn of the twentieth century, which allowed it to freely build up its cultural and scientific resources. Also, the United States' agricultural economy depended on the importation of crops native to other countries because the only major crop native to North America was the sunflower. [17]

Even the music for the U.S. national anthem, "The Star-Spangled Banner," was swiped from a popular eighteenth-century English song, "To Anacreon in Heaven." This old drinking song was written by a group of English dandies in the Anacreonic Club, which was devoted to an orgy-loving Greek bard who lived during the 500 b.c.e. era. (Little do people know when they patriotically sing the anthem at sports games that the tune originally celebrated Dionysian explosions of sex and drinking.) In 1812 lyricist Francis Scott Key borrowed the tune, and in 1931 it became the national anthem.[18] Then in 1969, at Woodstock, Jimi Hendrix famously reappropriated the anthem and drenched it in a purple haze of feedback that fit the violent and dissonant Vietnam era. We are a nation of pirates.

United States Pirate Party

Now the United States and other rich countries want strict enforcements of intellectual-property laws that ensure developing countries will remain uncompetitive within the globalized economy. Again, we wonder why much of the world hates us. Defenders of overbroad gene patents, terminator seeds, and global intellectual property treaties argue that without technologies and legal protections that safeguard their investments, there would be no incentive to develop new, innovative products. Companies such as Monsanto (whose comforting motto is "Food—Health—Hope") insist that their motivations for doing business are grounded in a desire to prevent world hunger. By creating more efficient products, biotech, agribusiness, and pharmaceutical companies can contribute to the betterment of humanity, they say.

However, if you buy that selfless line of reasoning, then I have a genetically altered monkey-boy I want to sell you (all sales final).

[This essay originally appeared in the author's book, *Freedom of Expression®* .]

KILLING THE CORPORATE PERSON
ANDREW "K'TETCH" NORTON

There's a quip which has become almost a statement of belief in recent years, "I will believe Corporations are people when Texas executes one." It's a statement that makes two points. First, Texas executes a lot of people, and has the lowest barrier of doing so, and secondly, that corporations are not people, because they don't face the same consequences that actual people do.

It captures a key essence in that corporations are people for any positive aspect, but not people for a negative one. If a company does wrong, its board isn't liable, unless they personally instructed and/or oversaw a criminal act. Instead, just the company is, and it only gets a financial penalty. This is as it should be, because that is the very reason for forming a company.

Let's take it down to basics. A company, when incorporated, is a limited liability company. That is its entire Raison d'être. It exists only to shield those behind a company from being liable for the company. How? Well, Anne and Bob open a shop. It sells cookers. They open it as a limited liability company, by incorporating. Charles and Denise open a shop next door, at the same time; they have a bed store. They decide not to incorporate.

The businesses run for 6 months and are just about making a profit (not an easy thing to do, since approximately 90% of businesses fail in the first year). They each buy a new delivery vehicle to help expand the business. 6 months after that, and disaster hits. A new superstore opens up just down the road, offering a wider range of both beds, AND cookers, at lower prices. They've been undercut and their businesses die. Both stores hang on for a month more, before going bankrupt. However, that's where the differences start.

Anne and Bob incorporated, so their business is a legal entity. It holds the debt. The store's lease belongs to the company, as does the loan on the delivery truck, and the money owed to their suppliers for the stock. These creditors can only pursue the company for the money. Anne and Bob's house, their car, bank accounts, etc. are all safe. All they've lost, or put at risk, is what they've put into the company.

Charles and Denise aren't so lucky; their company is only a partnership, which is an agreement between two people, and as such, they are responsible for the debts. Once the van and the stock has been sold off to pay what they owe, they'll have to cover any shortfall out of their own pockets. That means they could lose their house, car, savings, even their own bed, all because they didn't incorporate.

That's the benefit of a corporation. It becomes a legal entity that can operate as a party to contracts, including financial ones. The problem is that some people have taken that "legal entity" status, and expanded it, claiming that since people are legal entities, legal entities are therefore people. After all, companies can marry (mergers) split (spin-off), grow, sign contracts, sue, even file taxes (and maybe even pay them); they must be people, and hence we have the term "corporate personhood."

The problem is, companies are *not* people. They never have been. If a person dies, that person is dead. They can't be brought back to life, a corporation can. A person has a fixed lifespan, a company doesn't (The Japanese hotel company Nisiyama Onsen Keiunkan is over 1300 years old, for instance). If the company breaks the law, does the company go to jail? No. At worst, it would be shut down, and very little stops the people behind that old company from just starting a new company.

The idea that people and corporations are the same thing is clearly ludicrous, and yet that's not stopped people from trying to make it a reality. Part of the issue in the US stems from US law, which states[1] "In determining the meaning of any Act of Congress, unless the context indicates otherwise-- the words 'person' and 'whoever' include corporations, companies, associations, firms, partnerships, societies, and joint stock companies, as well as individuals."

This is extremely broad. The problem is, you can't put a corporation in jail, or execute it, so "in context," punishments tend not to apply. Who do you put in jail, how do you punish the company in a way that actually punishes, and while allowing it to continue operating?

Then there's the impact of corporate personhood on natural persons. In 2010, a 5-4 decision by the US Supreme Court[2] ruled that corporate persons have a first amendment right to advertise freely for candidates and issues. While corporations can't vote (with some exceptions, such as the election of the Lord Mayor of London), those employed by it can, and the direction taken by it, and the use of the company resources, are at the direction of the board, under nominal control of the shareholders (which are often other companies). The board not only has their own personal 1st amendment rights, and their own personal resources, but they can use the company resources to further their own personal interests.

Other issues are ones of morality, and punishment, exemplified in a document generally referred to as the Ford Pinto Memo. This was a document[3] submitted by the Ford Motor Company, to the National Highway Traffic Safety Administration – a Federal agency – amid concerns over the safety of the Ford Pinto's fuel tank in a crash. It contained a cost-benefit analysis which laid out the cost of modification to improve the safety of the car (12,500,000 vehicles at $11 a time, for a total of $137.5 million) against the costs of paying out-of-court settlements for accidents (which worked out to $49.53

million). Thus it was cheaper to send out cars that were potentially lethal, and pay out of court settlements. Were 'natural persons' (you and me) to attempt to knowingly sell defective products, we would potentially be looking at an involuntary (or criminally negligent) manslaughter charge. A company faces no such charges; but is instead usually charged with liability. The corporate person, quite literally, "gets away with murder."

Should a person's job give you two sets of rights, one for you, and one for the company?

Clearly not, as that does not make sense. So what can we do about it?

There are at least three schools of thought on this topic. They can be described as "take the rights," "adjusted punishments," and "Corporate Responsibility."

"Take the rights" is effectively ending corporate personhood as it is now. It can't be completely done away with, as it still needs the ability to make contracts, and perform acts requiring a legal entity. Instead it specifically narrows down the rights of a corporation. It clearly delineates the boundaries between natural people (those who are Homo sapiens and lawyers) and corporate persons, and the rights they have.

The second is to adjust punishments, so that corporations pay more. Even small companies have balance sheets that dwarf most natural people. So perhaps the model of punishment used in the north-west section of Europe (Finland, Sweden, Denmark, and Germany, among others) better known as Day Fines. These are fines based on income, with formulae to work out the specific person's fine amount-per-day, with the court sentence given in terms of days (and a minimum fine amount). Applied to a corporation, it would be a major deterrent, while punishing all companies evenly. It also avoids the current situation, where punishments are too low now to affect most corporations, while also being too high for individuals; a classic example being statutory copyright infringement damages. Set between $750 to $150,000 for willful infringement, to many companies that is not a major amount, whereas it's beyond the ability of most natural people.

The third option is corporate responsibility. In short, the board is directly responsible for the actions of the company, because the company doesn't have any rights, but instead shares the rights of the board of directors. The company itself has only two "rights," that of limited liability, and that of being a legal party to contracts. Anything else, including free speech, is down to the board or employees directly responsible.

These are just possibilities, but it's certainly something that needs to be looked at now, because companies are only getting bigger, and already the 5 biggest companies each have annual revenues bigger than the GDP of all but the top 35 countries (by IMF figures), while the biggest, Wal-Mart, would slot in at number 25, just ahead of Norway, and behind Taiwan at $421 billion/year.

While it might seem an 'anti-corporate' stance, the idea of corporations being "people" is not one that should be encouraged. Corporations were created to provide limited liability, and to be a single entity for contract law, nothing more. Ultimately, it comes to the following point: Slavery was about treating people as property, Corporate Personhood is about treating property as a person.

Trying to create artificial people, giving businesses advantages and no disadvantages, means they have disproportionate powers, and the bigger the company, the more power it has, until it's too big to fail, then we just keep bailing things out, and buckling under the influence. How is that in any way right?

Of course, there is always the Texas standard, mentioned earlier, and not believe Corporate Persons exist until Texas executes one.

PRIVACY

"REAL NAMES" POLICIES ARE AN ABUSE OF POWER
danah boyd

Everyone's abuzz with the "nymwars," mostly in response to Google Plus' decision to enforce its "real names" policy. At first, Google Plus went on a deleting spree, killing off accounts that violated its policy. When the community reacted with outrage, Google Plus leaders tried to calm the anger by detailing their "new and improved" mechanism to enforce "real names" (without killing off accounts). This only sparked increased discussion about the value of pseudonymity. Dozens of blog posts have popped up with people expressing their support for pseudonymity and explaining their reasons. One of the posts, by Kirrily "Skud" Robert included a list of explanations that came from people she polled, including:

• "I am a high school teacher, privacy is of the utmost importance."

• "I have used this name/account in a work context, my entire family knows this name and my friends know this name. It enables me to participate online without being subjected to harassment that at one point in time lead to my employer having to change their number so that calls could get through."

- "I do not feel safe using my real name online as I have had people track me down from my online presence and had coworkers invade my private life."

- "I've been stalked. I'm a rape survivor. I am a government employee that is prohibited from using my IRL."

- "As a former victim of stalking that impacted my family, I've used [my nickname] online for about 7 years."

- "[This name] is a pseudonym I use to protect myself. My web site can be rather controversial and it has been used against me once."

- "I started using [this name] to have at least a little layer of anonymity between me and people who act inappropriately/criminally. I think the "real names" policy hurts women in particular.

- "I enjoy being part of a global and open conversation, but I don't wish for my opinions to offend conservative and religious people I know or am related to. Also I don't want my husband's Government career impacted by his opinionated wife, or for his staff to feel in any way uncomfortable because of my views."

- "I have privacy concerns for being stalked in the past. I'm not going to change my name for a Google Plus page. The price I might pay isn't worth it."

- "We get death threats at the blog, so while I'm not all that concerned with, you know, sane people finding me. I just don't overly share information and use a pen name."

- "This identity was used to protect my real identity as I am gay and my family live in a small village where if it were openly known that their son was gay they would have problems."

- "I go by a pseudonym for safety reasons. Being female, I am wary of internet harassment."

You'll notice a theme here…

Another site has popped up called "My Name Is Me" where people vocalize their support for pseudonyms. What's most striking is the list of people who are affected by "real names" policies, including abuse survivors, activists, LGBT people, women, and young people.

Over and over again, people keep pointing to Facebook as an example where "real names" policies work. This makes me laugh hysterically. One of the things that became patently clear to me in my fieldwork is that countless teens who signed up to Facebook late into the game chose to use pseudonyms or nicknames. What's even more noticeable in my data is that an extremely high percentage of people of color used pseudonyms as compared to the white teens that I interviewed. Of course, this would make sense…

The people who most heavily rely on pseudonyms in online spaces are those who are most marginalized by systems of power. **"Real names" policies aren't empowering; they're an authoritarian assertion of power over vulnerable people.** These ideas and issues aren't new (and I've even talked about this before), but what is new is that marginalized people are banding together and speaking out loudly. And thank goodness.

What's funny to me is that people also don't seem to understand the history of Facebook's "real names" culture. When early adopters (first the elite college students…) embraced Facebook, it was a trusted community. They gave the name that they used in the context of college or high school or the corporation that they were a part of. They used the name that fit into the network that they joined Facebook with. The names they used weren't necessarily their legal names; plenty of people chose Bill instead of William. But they were, for all intents and purposes, "real." As the site grew larger, people had to grapple with new crowds being present and discomfort emerged over the norms. But the norms were set and people kept signing up and giving the name that they were most commonly known by. By the time celebrities kicked in, Facebook wasn't demanding that Lady Gaga call herself Stefani Germanotta, but of course, she had a "fan page" and was separate in the eyes of the crowd. Meanwhile, what many folks failed to notice is that countless black and Latino youth signed up to Facebook using handles. Most people don't notice what black and Latino youth do online. Likewise, people from outside of the US started signing up to Facebook and using alternate names. Again, no one noticed because names transliterated from Arabic or Malaysian or containing phrases in Portuguese weren't particularly visible to the real name enforcers. Real names are by no means universal on Facebook, but it's the importance of real names is a myth that Facebook likes to shill out. And, for the most part, privileged white Americans use their real name on Facebook. So it "looks" right.

Then along comes Google Plus, thinking that it can just dictate a "real names" policy. Only, they made a huge mistake. They allowed the tech crowd to join within 48 hours of launching. The thing about the tech crowd is that it has a long history of nicks and handles and pseudonyms. And this crowd got to define the early social norms of the site, rather than being socialized into the norms set up by trusting college students who had joined a site that they thought was college-only. This was not a recipe for "real name" norm setting. Quite the opposite. Worse for Google… Tech folks are VERY happy to speak LOUDLY when they're pissed off. So while countless black and Latino folks have been using nicks all over Facebook (just like they did on MySpace, by the way), they never loudly challenged Facebook's policy. There was more of a "live and let live" approach to this. Not so lucky for Google and its name-bending community. Folks are now PISSED OFF.

Personally, I'm ecstatic to see this much outrage. And I'm really really glad to see seriously privileged people take up the issue, because while they are the least likely to actually be harmed by "real names" policies, they have the authority to be able to speak truth to power. And across the web, I'm seeing people highlight that this issue has more depth to it than fun names (and is a whole lot more complicated than boiling it down to being about anonymity, as Facebook's Randi Zuckerberg foolishly did).

What's at stake is people's right to protect themselves, their right to actually maintain a form of control that gives them safety. **If companies like Facebook and Google are actually committed to the safety of its users, they need to take these complaints seriously.** Not everyone is safer by giving out their real name. Quite the opposite; many people are far LESS safe when they are identifiable. And those who are least safe are often those who are most vulnerable.

Likewise, the issue of reputation must be turned on its head when thinking about marginalized people. Folks point to the issue of people using pseudonyms to obscure their identity and, in theory, "protect" their reputation. The assumption baked into this is that the observer is qualified to actually assess someone's reputation. All too often, and especially with marginalized people, the observer takes someone out of context and judges them inappropriately based on what they get online. Let me explain this in a concrete example that many of you have heard before. Years ago, I received a phone call from an Ivy League college admissions officer who wanted to accept a young black man from South Central in LA into their college; the student had written an application about how he wanted to leave behind the gang-ridden community he came from, but the admissions officers had found his MySpace which was filled with gang insignia. The question that was asked of me was "Why would he lie to us when we can tell the truth online?" Knowing that community, I was fairly certain that he was being honest with the college; he was also doing what it took to keep himself alive in his community. If he had used a pseudonym, the college wouldn't have been able to get data out of context about him and inappropriately judge him. But they didn't. They thought that their frame mattered most. I really hope that he got into that school.

There is no universal context, no matter how many times geeks want to tell you that you can be one person to everyone at every point. But just because people are doing what it takes to be appropriate in different contexts, to protect their safety, and to make certain that they are not judged out of context, doesn't mean that everyone is a huckster. Rather, people are responsibly and reasonably responding to the structural conditions of these new media. And there's nothing acceptable about those who are most privileged and powerful telling those who aren't that it's OK for their safety to be undermined. And you don't guarantee safety by stopping people from using pseudonyms, but you do undermine people's safety by doing so.

Thus, from my perspective, enforcing "real names" policies in online spaces is an abuse of power.

[This article first appeared on the author's website at http://zephoria.org.]

CRIMINAL OF INNOCENCE
TRAVIS MCCREA

Charlie walked into class on Wednesday, like he did every Wednesday (and as he did every Monday, Tuesday, Thursday, and Friday as well). This was, however, not an average Wednesday, as after the announcements were over, a girl walked into his class room, and delivered a note to Mr. Wiener (pronounced Whiner, but this did not stop the junior class from making the jokes).

"This is going to be me, I just know it." Charlie said to himself. Of course, he said this to himself every time a note came into his class, as did every other student.

Charlie Wells was a 16 year old boy, who grew up in a small town in Kansas, just south of Topeka. A sandy haired boy, who had good grades, good friends, and was a good athlete. His favorite sport was wrestling, which had a meet coming up this Friday. Charlie was shorter than most of his classmates, but in general a high achiever. Rarely got in trouble at home, and never got in trouble at school (even won a student of the month award once).

"Mr. Wells," Mr. Wee-ner always seemed to have a condescending tone, he could tell someone they won the lottery, and they would instantly think of all the things their parents taught them about money. "You have been requested to the office by Mr. Jay."

Mr. Jay was the vice principal of the school, though typically the students call this position the "disciplinary principal" around adults. Though, when they were in private they would of course call him "Mr. BJ" due to high school students uncanny ability to find a sexual reference in anything.

"Will I need to take my stuff?" Charlie asked, as does every student who is being called out of the room, there should be a check box on the little slip that comes to the room… of course Mr. Wiener knows about as much about this trip to the office as Charlie does. Mr. Wiener simply told him to leave his stuff under his desk and he can get it after his meeting, and if class was over he would set it on the counter.
As annoying as Mr. Wiener was, Charlie always had a certain respect for him. Sure he sounded condescending, but Charlie's voice was still relatively high and he mocked himself that he sounded like a girl. That's not his fault as much as it was Wiener's for sounding like a dick (there it is again). Wiener always looked out for his students, and on more than one occasion has even wrote Charlie a late pass to his next class, just so he could stay and finish up some math problems, so he wouldn't have homework.

Charlie didn't even see the girl who brought the note leave, he must have been in the zone or just didn't care, but now as he walked to the office he wanted the company of that girl. He didn't even know her name, she looked like she might be a freshman, "How do you even become the office helper person?" he quietly thought to himself.

Charlie didn't want to talk to the girl because he was particularly attracted to her, though at his age he was attracted to anything with breasts, he simply wanted to stop thinking about what awaited him at the office."They caught me for using the proxy to check my Facespace account."

He turned the hall to the office.

"No, I was signed in under a guest account, they would have no way of knowing that."

Charlie entered the office, and smiled at the receptionist. She greeted him, and told him to take a seat and that Mr. Jay would be out to see him shortly. "The receptionist could have been working at Wal-Mart," Charlie thought to himself.

After sitting in the uncomfortable seat, trying to focus on reading old magazines which were probably scrounged from the library's discard pile, Charlie finally told himself that the best response to this situation was to have Mr. Jay tell him what he did wrong, and to only answer questions with short direct answers until this situation played out for him.

Charlie started to get a little frustrated, because it had been about ten minutes, and Mr. BJ (Charlie chuckled to himself), had not called him into his office. For a guy who cares about education, he sure was disrupting Charlie's class time... though of course Charlie was not concerned about his class, rather, he just didn't like stewing in his chair, not knowing what he did wrong.

As the door handle turned, Charlie jumped. Inside the room were the stern faces of Mr. Jay, and school resource officer (SRO), Officer Clark. Their eyes seared into his soul, like that of his mother's when she would catch him in a lie (which, admittedly, was not that often). He was ready to throw everything out the window and confess for everything he did, even the things he wasn't sure were against the rules like leaving Physical Education after he had already changed clothes, but before the bell like his classmates.

"Son," This was the only pet peeve Charlie had, the names "son," "buddy," "champ," "boss," etc. It wasn't necessary and made it seem as though the person was talking down to him. Of course in this situation, Mr. Jay was. "Do you know why you are here?"
Charlie knew he had to give them something, but thought he should start with something light. "I leave Physical Education a couple minutes early, so I can have some time to get to my locker before the bell rings?"

Officer Clark raised his eyebrow, and looked to Mr. Jay. However, Mr. Jay seemed to have been somehow offended by this answer, and raised his voice slightly "Charlie, we are not here to play games with you, what you did was serious, and if you do not cooperate with us… your punishment will be very severe.

Charlie didn't know what was going on, if he wasn't being yelled at he would have laughed and thought it was a joke. He tried to stammer out that he did not know what Mr Jay was talking about and so the SRO turned on the TV that had been behind them.

Charlie watched the screen, as he watched himself come around the "C" hallway, which was the furthest hallway running horizontally cutting though the two main hallways in that wing of the school, and walk down main hallway 2 until he was out of the frame.

Charlie was very confused at this point, and asked "Can you please explain to me what this is?"

Mr. Jay was very upset at this point and explained to Charlie that he had given him plenty of chances to explain himself, and that he had pushed his patience to the limit. Jay further went on to explain that there was a bag of pot found in that hall at the end of that period, and that Charlie had been the only student to have been using the hall.

"Sir, this must be a misunderstanding," Charlie exclaimed, nervously "I don't even smoke pot, I don't think any of my friends do either!"

"Charlie, why would you be walking down that hallway at that time? You were supposed to be in Science, and that's on the other wing of school. The only class you had down that way was your math class, and it had been a couple periods before." Officer Clark seemed to talk much more reasonably; however, he too stared at Charlie like he was a criminal. Heck in their eyes he WAS a criminal.

"I left my binder in Math class, I didn't need it in any of my other classes after Math, and so I went back to get it so I could turn in an assignment for Science." Charlie felt guilty, like he really had done something wrong. That feeling like going through US Customs trying to re-enter his country, where after you tell them the trip was for pleasure, they ask what kind of pleasure, what did you do, how long… to the point you start questioning it yourself.

"I am growing tired of your lies, Mr. Wells," Back to Mr. Jay ('was this some form of bad cop, worse cop?' Charlie was thinking to himself). "We had spoken with Mr. Wiener, and he insisted that you never came by his class… and also if you look at that video there is no binder."

Charlie was so scared, he should have been frustrated… of course he should have been, but he didn't get frustrated. Heck, he hadn't even cared when they put up these dumb cameras. He didn't do anything wrong so there was no fear of him getting in trouble for them… so he thought.

Charlie explained that he saw Mr. Wiener was instructing his class, so he decided to get his binder later. This caused Mr. Jay to believe that he was changing his story, and decided this was enough cause to search his locker for drugs.

As Charlie, Officer Clark, and Mr. Jay reached his locker, the end-of-period bell rang, and all the students flooded the halls. Charlie didn't realize how many students there were in his school, or how many went by his locker, until every single one of them were staring at him.

More embarrassment came to Charlie as he opened his locker. All the things that had seemed funny, stupid, or weird that he had put in the door of his locker, now seemed much worse when he had the cop and disciplinary principal behind him. Charlie could just feel the eyes burning into the back of his neck, knowing they were judging him for the picture of the midget swimsuit model, or the comic about teachers running off a cliff after a penny.

They didn't find anything in Charlie's locker. However, it was not over for Charlie. The principal gave him a day of in-school suspension for wandering the halls, and the resource officer called Charlie's parents to tell them that their son had been suspected of at the very least being in possession of marijuana, and potentially distributing it.

United States Pirate Party

After this whole ordeal, it had changed Charlie into a very anti-authoritarian person, he had started putting tape up over the cameras, and fighting (to a degree some would consider excess) for the rights of other students, even ones he didn't know. Charlie would tell the other students, "I thought that as long as I would go with the system, I would never have to worry about rights, or any of that stuff, I was wrong. Even the innocent are treated as guilty in a system that takes away rights. If the system wants to treat innocent people like criminals, well then I am going to be a criminal."

[This story was originally published on the author's website at http://travismccrea.com.]

PRIVACY NOW, NOTHING LATER
RYAN MOFFITT

Let me propose a scenario for you. I'd say close your eyes, but you might need them to read said proposal:

Imagine living in a world where you are photographed at practically every street corner. Imagine living in a world where every time you check your email or search for a recipe, it's recorded and stored in a database. Imagine living in a world where tracking devices record and report your every movement. Imagine living in a world where you have to stop and wonder who may be watching or listening.

Sounds like a scary place from an Orwell novel or some dark third-world corner of the planet, doesn't it? Many of us can't actually imagine living in a world where privacy is just a word. Luckily for those people, they don't have to imagine such a dystopia. They just have to wake up in the morning. We experience this world every day. Data retention laws exist, GPS tracking devices have been installed and used by intelligence agencies, and the average person is recorded by CCTV and other surveillance equipment over 300 times a day. This is all happening right here, in the developed world, and it doesn't seem to bother people in the slightest.

Think about what you depend on privacy for. When you go to vote on election day, you vote for the person you want to vote for because you know the ballot is secret. Nobody will know who got your vote, and it doesn't get traced back to you. When you are with your partner, you know that what goes on behind closed doors is your own business. You hope that when you send an email, text or other form of instant message, your intended recipient will receive that message in confidence, allowing you to express yourself freely and openly. Government and corporate whistle-blowers depend on privacy and confidentiality to protect themselves after exposing wrong-doing. Without privacy, your entire world can be flipped upside down, and chances are you may not even notice.

But before we start marching on Washington, we must consider another issue: Big Brother doesn't have to be the one watching, and that information doesn't have to be forcibly taken.

"We know where you are. We know where you've been. We can more or less know what you're thinking."

-Eric Schmidt, CEO of Google, Inc.

When talking about loss of privacy, governments and people in power are usually the first to be blamed, and rightfully so. However, you can either knowingly or inadvertently volunteer more information to surveillance-friendly corporations who will pass it along to Big Brother than Big Brother himself could reasonably take from you. Companies like Google and Facebook have voluntarily turned over personal information about criminal suspects and activists, without ever so much as asking for a warrant, and without the targeted people being notified of the leak. It's pointless to demand the end of surveillance without demanding the end of corporate cooperation.

So what does this all mean? Are we doomed to a future where there are cameras in your dashboard and your email comes with a 3kb attachment stating your message is "Department of Homeland Security Approved"? It depends. The ordinary citizen may view a bad privacy policy or a new airport screening measure as a small sacrifice. The future will lie in just how much the masses are willing to sacrifice.

PERSONAL PRIVACY
TRAVIS MCCREA

Privacy is a funny issue for a lot of people, they are so willing to yield so much of their privacy to people who tell them it's for "their safety," yet will squawk like a chicken if they find out that their public posts to Twitter are being indexed by a company (or a government entity). I have found (and I think many already know this) that the general public is highly susceptible to fear mongers, and when they are told that something is bad or out to get them, they listen intently and then throw their arms up in the air not knowing exactly what is wrong, but that it is wrong and that they are against it. The government says that Homeland Security has to do full body scans of people as they try to board an airplane because it will protect from bad people getting on an aircraft and blowing it up, what they don't tell you is that now every time you want to board an aircraft, someone gets to look at you naked.

I, myself, could be viewed as someone who treats his privacy with little regard online. You can do a quick Google search of "Travis McCrea" and find my phone number, full name, background, and if you search hard enough, some of my previous addresses. I also have a Gmail account which is operated by the "evil" Google Inc., hell I even have a Facebook page that lets almost anyone view my information. I do this because it was already out there, if I give my phone number to even a couple people online, I have pretty much committed it to the public domain. Since I already know that at that point someone who wants to harm me by obtaining my phone number, can already get it... I might as well make it easier for the good people who want to call me as well.

Here is the difference between Travis McCrea, and Joe Blow off the street when it comes to digital privacy: I know that everything I post online is viewable by the world. If I don't want the world to see it, rarely do I ever even say it online (not even in private). However, I do still maintain the tools necessary to facilitate a private conversation if I must... and I do use them. When I use tools that I expect to be anonymous, I will use TOR (which isn't exactly privacy guarding either). As much random stuff I search, I have never found a need to use haystacking or anything like that... I use https://www.google.com and that makes me feel good enough.

Most people will point out as well that I trust Google a lot, and I am a self-labeled Google fanboy and I am okay with that. I can see the argument of, "sure you can trust Google now, but can you trust them in 30 years?", but I also am sure that Google understands that putting the interests of its customers over the interests of governments or other corporations is a better business model. Yes, they have made calls in the past that I have disapproved of... but again it's an understanding: I accept that Google gives me cool free stuff, if I am willing to give them anonymous pieces of information about myself. Google honestly does not even have the man-power to read .001% of the emails that are sent every day if it wanted to. It may turn data over to the police if subpoenaed, but they do the best job at reporting legal notices and government requests than any other major service provider I have seen. Even searches alone, who else are you going to trust with your data? Microsoft?

The biggest fear of corporations is that they sell your information to other corporations, or lose your information to hackers in a worst-case-scenario. The biggest fear of government is that they come to your house, take you away, erase all your evidence of being born, tell people you are a terrorist, and never give you a fair trial. I am not saying give full confidence to corporations either. Corporations have very little restrictions as to how they must handle the private information of its customers. They don't HAVE to MD5 sum your passwords, or encrypt your personal data in their database, some do, just to protect their customers. Others don't care. Some companies do things to try and help their users with simpler interfaces, and actually enable their customers to easily give up their privacy. I think this is what happened to Facebook: They had no intentions on being evil by making people's information show up to everyone by default, they were simply making it easier for their members to find each other… however, their default settings put anyone who created an account at risk of potential employers and ex-girl/boyfriends stalking them.

The main point, is that it's very important for people to understand exactly what is happening with their information. Read through the privacy agreement, and if it's in legalese I encourage you to email the website, company, etc. and ask them to explain your rights, and what steps you can do to protect your privacy, and what steps they take to protect it. Twitter does a very good job of explaining each line of legalese in plain English if you read their privacy policy.

Remind your friends how important it is to protect their privacy, and when you hear people spouting off about "national security," ask them if they mind if you go look through their underwear drawer due to "national security." It's your patriotic duty to stand up against a government who treats its citizens as the enemy, and say that you will not accept it anymore.

Fight the fight, be a patriot of our digital revolution.

[This story was originally published on the author's website at http://travismccrea.com.]

NOTES ON THE FOURTH AMENDMENT
THE ELECTRONIC FRONTIER FOUNDATION

The Fourth Amendment

The Fourth Amendment says, "[t]he right of the people to be secure in their persons, houses, papers, and effects, against unreasonable searches and seizures, shall not be violated, and no Warrants shall issue, but upon probable cause, supported by Oath or affirmation, and particularly describing the place to be searched, and the persons or things to be seized."

A seizure occurs when the government takes possession of items or detains people.

A search is any intrusion by the government into something in which one has a reasonable expectation of privacy.

Some examples of searches include: reaching into your pockets or searching through your purse; entering into your house, apartment, office, hotel room, or mobile home; and examining the contents of your backpack or luggage. Depending on the facts, eavesdropping on your conversations or wiretapping of your communications can also constitute a search and seizure under the Fourth Amendment.

The Fourth Amendment requires searches and seizures to be "reasonable", which generally means that police must get a search warrant if they want to conduct a legal search or seizure, although there are exceptions to this general rule. If a search or seizure is "unreasonable" and thus illegal, then police cannot use the evidence obtained through that search or seizure in a criminal trial. This is called the exclusionary rule and it is the primary incentive against government agents violating your Fourth Amendment rights.

A few important things to remember:

The Fourth Amendment protects you from unreasonable searches whether or not you are a citizen. In particular, the exclusionary rule applies to all criminal defendants, including non-citizens. However, the exclusionary rule does not apply in immigration hearings, meaning that the government may introduce evidence from an illegal search or seizure in those proceedings.

The Fourth Amendment applies whenever the government — whether local, state or federal — conducts a search or seizure. It protects you from an unreasonable search or seizure by any government official or agent, not just the police.

The Fourth Amendment does not protect you from privacy invasions by people other than the government, even if they later hand over what they found to the government — unless the government directed them to search your things in the first place.

Your Fourth Amendment rights against unreasonable searches and seizures cannot be suspended — even during a state of emergency or wartime — and they have not been suspended by the USA PATRIOT Act or any other post-9/11 legislation.

No Safe Harbor

If you are ever searched or served with any kind of government order, contact a lawyer immediately to discuss your rights. Contact a lawyer any time you are searched, threatened with a search, or served with any kind of legal papers from the government or anyone else. If you do not have a lawyer, pro bono legal organizations such as EFF are available to help you or assist in finding other lawyers who will.

The Fourth Amendment only protects you against searches that violate your reasonable expectation of privacy. A reasonable expectation of privacy exists if 1) you actually expect privacy, and 2) your expectation is one that society as a whole would think is legitimate.

This rule comes from a decision by the United States Supreme Court in 1967. Katz v. United States, holding that when a person enters a telephone booth, shuts the door, and makes a call, the government can not record what that person says on the phone without a warrant. Even though the recording device was stuck to the outside of the phone booth glass and did not physically invade Katz's private space, the Supreme Court decided that when Katz shut the phone booth's door, he justifiably expected that no one would hear his conversation, and that it was this expectation — rather than the inside of the phone booth itself — that was protected from government intrusion by the Fourth Amendment. This idea is generally phrased as "the Fourth Amendment protects people, not places."

A big question in determining whether your expectation of privacy is "reasonable" and protected by the Fourth Amendment arises when you have "knowingly exposed" something to another person or to the public at large. Although Katz did have a reasonable expectation of privacy in the sound of his conversation, would he have had a reasonable expectation of privacy in his appearance or actions while inside the glass phone booth? Probably not.

Thus, some Supreme Court cases have held that you have no reasonable expectation of privacy in information you have "knowingly exposed" to a third party — for example, bank records or records of telephone numbers you have dialed — even if you intended for that third party to keep the information secret. In other words, by engaging in transactions with your bank or communicating phone numbers to your phone company for the purpose of connecting a call, you've "assumed the risk" that they will share that information with the government.

You may "knowingly expose" a lot more than you really know or intend. Most information a third party collects — such as your insurance records, credit records, bank records, travel records, library records, phone records and even the records your grocery store keeps when you use your "loyalty" card to get discounts — was given freely to them by you, and is probably not protected by the Fourth Amendment under current law. There may be privacy statutes that protect against the sharing of information about you — some communications records receive special legal protection, for example — but there is likely no constitutional protection, and it is often very easy for the government to get a hold of these third party records without your ever being notified.

Here are some more details on how the Fourth Amendment will — or won't — protect you in certain circumstances:

Residences. Everyone has a reasonable expectation of privacy in their home. This is not just a house as it says in the Fourth Amendment, but anywhere you live, be it an apartment, a hotel or motel room, or a mobile home.

However, even things in your home might be knowingly exposed to the public and lose their Fourth Amendment protection. For example, you have no reasonable expectation of privacy in conversations or other sounds inside your home that a person outside could hear, or odors that a passerby could smell (although the Supreme Court has held that more invasive technological means of obtaining information about the inside of your home, like thermal imaging technology to detect heat sources, is a Fourth Amendment search requiring a warrant). Similarly, if you open your house to the public for a party, a political meeting, or some other public event, police officers could walk in posing as guests and look at or listen to whatever any of the other guests could, without having to get a warrant.

Business premises. You have a reasonable expectation of privacy in your office, so long as it's not open to the public. But if there is a part of your office where the public is allowed, like a reception area in the front, and if a police officer enters that part of the office as any other member of the public is allowed to, it is not a search for the officer to look at objects in plain view or listen to conversations there. That's because you've knowingly exposed that part of your office to the public. However, if the officer does not stay in that portion of the premises that is open to the public — if he starts opening file cabinets or tries to go to private offices in the back without an invitation — then his conduct becomes a search requiring a search warrant.

Trash. The things you leave outside your home at the edge of your property are unprotected by the Fourth Amendment. For example, once you carry your trash out of your house or office and put it on the curb or in the dumpster for collection, you have given up any expectation of privacy in the contents of that trash. You should always keep this in mind when you are disposing of sensitive documents or anything else that you want to keep private. You may want to shred all paper documents and destroy all electronic media. You could also try to put the trash out (or unlock your trashcan) right before it's picked up, rather than leaving it out overnight without a lock.

Public places. It may sound obvious, but you have little to no privacy when you are in public. When you are in a public place — whether walking down the sidewalk, shopping in a store, sitting in a restaurant or in the park — your actions, movements, and conversations are knowingly exposed to the public. That means the police can follow you around in public and observe your activities, see what you are carrying or to whom you are talking, sit next to you or behind you and listen to your conversations — all without a warrant. You cannot necessarily expect Fourth Amendment protection when you're in a public place, even if you think you are alone. Fourth Amendment challenges have been unsuccessfully brought against police officers using monitoring beepers to track a suspect's location in a public place, but it is unclear how those cases might apply to more pervasive remote monitoring, like using GPS or other cell phone location information to track a suspect's physical location.

Infiltrators and undercover agents. Public meetings of community and political organizations, just like any other public places, are not private. If the government considers you a potential criminal or terrorist threat, or even if they just have an unfounded suspicion that your organization might be up to something, undercover police or police informants could come to your public meetings and attempt to infiltrate your organization. They may even wear hidden microphones and record every word that's said. Investigators can lie about their identities and never admit that they're cops — even if asked directly. By infiltrating your organization, the police can identify any of your supporters, learn about your plans and tactics, and could even get involved in the politics of the group and influence organizational decisions. You may want to save the open-to-the-public meetings for public education and other non-sensitive matters and only discuss sensitive matters in meetings limited to the most trusted, long-time staff and constituents.

Importantly, the threat of infiltrators exists in the virtual world as well as the physical world: for example, a police officer may pose as a online "friend" in order to access your private social network profile.

Records stored by others. As the Supreme Court has stated, "The Fourth Amendment does not prohibit the obtaining of information revealed to a third party and conveyed by him to Government authorities, even if the information is revealed on the assumption that it will be used only for a limited purpose and the confidence placed in the third party will not be betrayed." This means that you will often have no Fourth Amendment protection in the records that others keep about you, because most information that a third party will have about you was either given freely to them by you, thus knowingly exposed, or was collected from other, public sources. It doesn't necessarily matter if you thought you were handing over the information in confidence, or if you thought the information was only going to be used for a particular purpose.

Therefore it is important to pay close attention to the kinds of information about you and your organization's activities that you reveal to third parties, and work to reduce the amount of private information you leave behind when you go about your daily business.

Opaque containers and packages. Even when you are in public, you have a reasonable expectation of privacy in the contents of any opaque (not see-through) clothes or containers. So, unless the police have a warrant or qualify for one of the warrantless search exceptions discussed below, they can't go digging in your pockets or rummaging through your bags.

Laptops, pagers, cell phones and other electronic devices are also protected. Courts have generally treated electronic devices that hold data as if they were opaque containers.

However, always keep in mind that whatever you expose to the public isn't protected. So, if you're in a coffee shop using your laptop and an FBI agent sitting at the next table sees what you are writing in an email, or if you open your backpack and the FBI agent can see what's inside, the Fourth Amendment won't protect you.

Postal mail. The mail that you send through the U.S. Postal Service is protected by the Fourth Amendment, and police have to get a warrant to open it in most cases.

If you're using the U.S. Postal Service, send your package using First Class mail or above. Postal inspectors don't need a search warrant to open discount (media) rate mail because it isn't supposed to be used for personal correspondence.

Keep in mind that although you have privacy in the contents of your mail and packages, you don't have any privacy in the "to" and "from" addresses printed on them. That means the police can ask the post office to report the name and address of every person you send mail to or receive mail from — this is called a "mail cover" — without getting a warrant. Mail covers are a low-tech form of "traffic analysis," which we'll discuss in the section dealing with electronic surveillance.

You don't have any privacy in what you write on a postcard, either. By not putting your correspondence in an envelope, you've knowingly exposed it, and the government can read it without a warrant.

Police at the door: Police in your home or office when it's open to the public?

The police may be able to come into your home or office if you have opened those places to the public — but you can also ask them to leave, just as if they were any other members of the public. If they don't have a warrant, or don't qualify for any of the warrant exceptions, they have no more right to stay once you've asked them to leave than any other trespasser. However, undercover agents or officers need not announce their true identities, so asking all cops to leave the room before a meeting is not going provide any protection..

Search Warrants Are Generally Required For Most Searches and Seizures.

The Fourth Amendment requires that any search or seizure be reasonable. The general rule is that warrantless searches or seizures are automatically unreasonable, though there are many exceptions.

To get a warrant, investigators must go to a neutral and detached magistrate and swear to facts demonstrating that they have probable cause to conduct the search or seizure. There is probable cause to search when a truthful affidavit establishes that evidence of a crime will probably be found in the particular place to be searched. Police suspicions or hunches aren't enough — probable cause must be based on actual facts that would lead a reasonable person to believe that the police will find evidence of a crime.

In addition to satisfying the Fourth Amendment's probable cause requirement, search warrants must satisfy the particularity requirement. This means that in order to get a search warrant, the police have to give the judge details about where they are going to search and what kind of evidence they are searching for. If the judge issues the search warrant, it will only authorize the police to search those particular places for those particular things.

Police at the door: Search warrants.

What should you do if a police officer comes to your home or office with a search warrant?

Be polite. Do not get in the officers' way, do not get into an argument with them or complain, even if you think your rights are being violated. Never insult a police officer. But you should say "I do not consent to this search." If they are properly authorized, they will search anyway. But if they are not, then you have reserved your right to challenge the search later.

Ask to see the warrant. You have a right to examine the warrant. The warrant must tell in detail the places to be searched and the people or things to be seized, and may limit what time of day the police can search. A valid warrant must have a recent date (usually not more than a couple of weeks), the correct address, and a judge's or magistrate's signature. If the warrant appears incomplete, indicates a different address, or otherwise seems mistaken, politely point this out to the police.

Clearly state that you do not consent to the search. The police don't need your consent if they have a warrant, but clearly saying "I do not consent to this search" will limit them to search only where the warrant authorizes. If possible, have witnesses around when you say it.

Do not resist, even if you think the search is illegal, or else you may be arrested. Keep your hands where the police can see them, and never touch a police officer. Do not try to leave if the police tell you to stay — a valid warrant gives them the right to detain any people that are on the premises while the search is conducted. You are allowed to observe and take notes of what the officers do, though they may tell you to sit in one place while they are conducting the search.

Don't answer any questions. The Fifth Amendment guarantees your right not to answer questions from the police, even if they have a warrant. Remember that anything you say might be used against you later. If they ask you anything other than your name and address, you should tell them "I choose to remain silent, and will not answer any questions without a lawyer." If you say this, they are legally required to stop asking you questions until you have a lawyer with you.

Take notes. Write down the police officers' names and badge numbers, as well as the names and contact information of any witnesses. Write down, as best you can remember, everything that the police say and everything you say to them. Ask if you can watch the search, and if they say yes, write down everything that you see them search and/or seize (you may also try to tape or take pictures, but realize that this may escalate the situation). If it appears they are going beyond what is authorized by the warrant, politely point this out.

Ask for an inventory. At the conclusion of the search, the police should typically provide an inventory of what has been seized; if not, request a copy but do not sign any statement that the inventory is accurate or complete.

Call a lawyer as soon as possible. If you don't have a lawyer, you can call EFF and we'll try to find you one.

Police at the door: Computer searches and seizures.

If the police believe a computer is itself evidence of a crime — for example, if it is stolen or was used to commit a crime — they will usually seize it and then search its contents later. However, if the evidence is just stored on the computer — for example, you have computer records that contain information about the person they are investigating — instead of seizing the whole machine, the police may choose to:

Search the computer and print out a hard copy of the particular files they are looking for (this is rarely done)

Search the computer and make an electronic copy of the particular files

Create a duplicate electronic copy of all of the computer's contents (this is called "imaging" or creating a "bitstream copy" of the computer hard drive) and then search for the particular files later

"Sneak and Peek" Search Warrants Are Easier to Obtain Than They Used to Be

Generally, police officers serving a warrant must "knock and announce" — that is, give you notice that they are the police and are serving a warrant (although they might not do this if they reasonably suspect that they will be put in danger, or that evidence will be destroyed, if they give such notice). If they have a warrant, they can enter and search even if you aren't home — but they still have to leave a copy of the warrant and an inventory of what they seized, so you'll know that your place was searched.

However, thanks to the USA PATRIOT Act, it is much easier for law enforcement to get permission from the court to delay notice rather than immediately inform the person whose premises are searched, if agents claim that giving notice would disrupt the investigation. Since the goal is not to tip the suspect off, these orders usually don't authorize the government to actually seize any property — but that won't stop them from poking around your computers.

The delay of notice in criminal cases can last months. The average delay is 30 to 90 days. In the case of super-secret foreign intelligence surveillance to be discussed later, the delay lasts forever — no one is ever notified, unless and until evidence from the search is introduced in open court.

The risk of being targeted with such a "sneak-and-peek" warrant is very low, although rising quickly. Law enforcement made 47 sneak-and-peek searches nationwide from September 2001 to April 2003 and an additional 108 through January 2005, averaging about fifty per year, mostly in drug cases. We don't know how many foreign intelligence searches there are per year — it's secret, of course — but we'd guess that it's much more common than secret searches by regular law enforcement.

Secret searches can be used to install eavesdropping and wiretapping devices. Secret searches may also be used to install a key-logging device on your computer. A key-logger records all of the keystrokes that you make on the computer's keyboard, for later retrieval by the police who installed it. So if you are concerned about government surveillance, you should check your office computers for new added hardware that you don't recognize — especially anything installed between the keyboard and the computer — and remove it. A hardware key-logger often looks like a little dongle in between the keyboard plug and computer itself. Keyghost is an example of a hardware key-logger.

However, the government also has the capability to remotely install software key-loggers on your computer — or search the contents of your hard drive, or install surveillance capability on your computer — using its own spyware. There were rumors of such capability a few years ago in news reports about a government software program code-named "Magic Lantern" that could be secretly installed and monitored over the Internet, without the police ever having to enter your house or office. More recently, news reports revealed that the government had in one case been able to hack into a computer remotely and install software code-named "CIPAV" (the "Computer and Internet Protocol Address Verifier"), which gave the government the IP addresses with which the infected computer communicated.

In response to a survey, all of the major anti-spyware companies claimed that their products would treat government spyware like any other spyware programs, so you should definitely use some anti-spyware product to monitor your computer for such programs. It's possible that a spyware company may receive a court order requiring it not to alert you to the presence of government spyware (several of the companies that were surveyed declined to say whether they had received such orders), but you should still use anti-spyware software if only to protect yourself against garden-variety spyware deployed by identity thieves and commercial data harvesters.

There Are Many Fourth Amendment Exceptions to the General Rule of Warrants

In some cases, a search can be reasonable — and thus allowed under the Fourth Amendment — even if the police don't have a warrant. There are several key exceptions to the warrant requirement that you should be aware of.

Consent. The police can conduct a warrantless search if you voluntarily consent to the search — that is, if you say it's OK. In fact, any person who the police reasonably think has a right to use or occupy the property, like a roommate or guest in your home, or a coworker at your office, can consent to the search. You can make clear to the people you share a home or office with that they do not have your permission to consent to a search and that if police ask, they should say no.

Privacy tip: Don't accidentally consent!

If the police show up at your door without a warrant, step outside then close and lock the door behind you — if you don't, they might just walk in, and later argue that you implied an invitation by leaving the door open. If they ask to come in, tell them "I do not consent to a search." Tell roommates, guests, coworkers and renters that they cannot consent on your behalf.

Administrative searches. In some cases, the government can conduct administrative searches. These are searches done for purposes other than law enforcement; for example, for a fire inspection. Court authorization is required for involuntary administrative searches, although the standards are lower. The only time the government doesn't need a warrant for an administrative search is when they are searching businesses in highly regulated industries such as liquor, guns, strip mining, waste management, nuclear power, etc. This exception to the warrant requirement clearly does not apply to the average homeowner, activist organization or community group.

Privacy tip: Just because they're "inspectors" doesn't mean you have to let them in!

If someone shows up at your home or office claiming to be a fire inspector, building code inspector, or some other non-law enforcement government employee who wants to inspect the premises, you can tell them to come back with a warrant. You don't have to let them in without a warrant!

Exigent circumstances. Exigent circumstances are emergency situations where it would be unreasonable for the police to wait to get a warrant, like if a person is calling for help from inside your house, if the police are chasing a criminal suspect who runs into an office or home, or if evidence will be destroyed if the police do not act immediately.

Privacy tip: Don't get tricked into consenting!

Police could try to get your consent by pressuring you, or making you think that you have to let them in. For example, they may show up at your door claiming that your neighbor saw someone breaking into your home or office, saw a criminal suspect entering the premises, or heard calls for help, and that they need to take a look around. You should never physically interfere if they demand to come in (which they will do if there are indeed exigent circumstances), but no matter what they say or do, keep saying the magic words: "I do not consent to a search."

Plain view. The police can make a warrantless search or seizure if they are lawfully in a position to see and access the evidence, so long as that evidence is obviously incriminating. For example, if the police enter a house with a valid search warrant to search for and seize some stolen electronics and then see a bag of drugs in plain view on the coffee table, they can seize the drugs too, even though the warrant didn't specifically authorize that seizure. Similarly, the police could seize the drugs without a warrant, or look at any other documents or things left in plain view in the house, if there were exigent circumstances that led the police into the house — for example, if a suspect they were chasing ran into the house, or if they heard gunshots from inside. Even a law-abiding citizen who does not have any contraband or evidence that the police would want to seize may still have sensitive documents in plain view that one would not want the authorities to see.

The plain view exception alone does not allow the police to enter your home or office without a warrant. So, for example, even if the police see evidence through your window, they cannot enter and seize it. However, plain view can combine with other exceptions to allow searches that might otherwise require a warrant. For example, if the person with the bag of drugs in the previous example saw the police looking through his window, then grabbed the bag and ran towards the bathroom as if he was about to flush the evidence down the toilet, that would be an exigent circumstance and the police could enter without a warrant to stop him.

Automobiles. Since cars and other vehicles are mobile, and therefore might not be around later if the police need to go get a warrant, the police can search them without one. They still need probable cause, though, because you do have a privacy interest in your vehicle.

If the police have probable cause, they can search the entire vehicle (including the trunk) and all containers in the vehicle that might contain the object for which they are searching. For example, if the police have probable cause to believe that drugs are in the vehicle, they can search almost any container, but if they have probable cause to believe that a murder suspect is hiding inside the vehicle, they must limit their search to areas where a person can hide.

Also, it's important to know that the "plain view" exception is often applied to cars. That means that the police aren't conducting a search just by looking through your car windows, or even by shining a flashlight in your car. And if they see evidence inside your car, that can then give them probable cause to search the rest of the vehicle under the automobile exception.

Police at the (car) door: What if I get pulled over?

If you are pulled over by a police officer, you may choose to stop somewhere you feel safe, both from traffic and from the officer herself. In other words, you can pull into a lighted gas station, or in front of someone's home or somewhere there are other people present, rather than stopping on a dark road, so long as you indicate to the officer by your driving that you are in fact stopping. You are required to show the officer your license, insurance and registration. Keep your hands where the officer can see them at all times. For example, you can wait to get your documentation out when the officer is standing near your car so that she can watch what you are doing and have no cause to fear that you are going into the glove box for a weapon. Be polite and courteous.

Airport searches. As you certainly know if you've flown recently, the government is allowed to search you and all your luggage for bombs and weapons before you are allowed to board a plane, without a warrant. Always assume that the government will look in your bags when you fly, and pack accordingly.

Border searches. The government has the right to warrantlessly search travelers at the border, including international airports, as part of its traditional power to control the flow of items into and out of the country. The case law distinguishes between "routine" searches, which require no cause, and "non-routine" searches, which require reasonable suspicion, but no warrant. "Non-routine" searches include strip searches, cavity searches, involuntary X-rays and other particularly invasive investigative techniques. Several courts have found that searching the contents of your laptop or other electronic devices is "routine" and doesn't require a warrant or even reasonable suspicion.

One solution to this problem is to bring a blank "traveling" laptop and leave your personal information at home. You could then access the information that you left at home over the internet by using a VPN or other secure method to connect to a server where you've stored the information.

However, bringing a clean laptop means more than simply dragging files into the trash. Deleting files will not remove them from your hard drive. See our software and technology article on secure deletion for details.

Another solution is to use password-based disk encryption to prevent border agents from being able to read your files. The consequences of refusing to disclose a password under those circumstances are difficult to predict with certainty, but non-citizens would face a significant risk of being refused entry to the country. Citizens cannot be refused entry, but could be detained until the border agents decide what to do, which may include seizing your computer.

Stop and frisk searches. The police can stop you on the street and perform a limited "pat-down" search or "frisk" — this means they can feel around your outer clothing for concealed weapons.

The police don't need probable cause to stop and frisk you, but they do at least need to have a reasonable suspicion of criminal activity based on specific facts. This is a very low standard, though, and the courts usually give the police a lot of leeway. For example, if a police officer is suspicious that you're carrying a concealed weapon based on the shape of a lump under your jacket or the funny way that you're walking, that's usually enough.

If, while patting you down, a police officer feels something that he reasonably believes is a weapon or an illegal item, the officer can reach into your clothes and seize that item. Search Incident to Lawful Arrest

Search Incident to Arrest (SITA) doctrine is an exception to the general requirement that police obtain a warrant before conducting a search. The purpose of this exception is to protect the officer by locating and seizing any weapons the person has and to prevent the destruction of any evidence on the person. According to the SITA doctrine, if an arrest is valid, officers may conduct a warrantless search of the arrestee and the area and objects in close proximity — i.e. the "grab area" — at about the same time as the arrest.

Officers may also perform inventory searches of the arrested person at the time of the arrest or upon arrival at the jail or other place of detention.

So, the police are allowed to search your clothing and your personal belongings after they've arrested you. They can also search any area nearby where you might conceal a weapon or hide evidence. If you are arrested inside a building, this usually means they can search the room they found you in but not the entire building. If you are arrested while driving, this means they can search inside the car, but not the trunk. But if they impound the car, then they can search the trunk as part of an inventory search. This is another example of the way that multiple exceptions to the warrant requirement can combine to allow the police a lot of leeway to search without going to a judge first.

When searches are delayed until some time after the arrest, courts generally have allowed warrantless searches of the person, including containers the arrestee carries, while rejecting searches of possessions that were within an arrestee's control. These no longer present any danger to the officer or risk of destruction because the arrestee is now in custody.

The question remains whether the SITA doctrine authorizes warrantless searches of the data on cell phones and computers carried by or located near the arrestee. There are very few cases addressing this question. In one case in Kansas, for example, the arresting officer downloaded the memory from the arrestee's cellphone for subsequent search. The court found that this seizure did not violate the Fourth Amendment because the officer only downloaded the dialed and incoming numbers, and because it was imperative to preserve the evidence given the volatile, easily destroyed, nature of cell phone memory.

In contrast, in another case in California, the court held that a cellphone search was not justified by the SITA doctrine because it was conducted for investigatory reasons rather than out of a concern for officer safety, or to prevent the concealment or destruction of evidence. The officers could seize the phone, and then go obtain a warrant to do any searching of it. The decision rejected the idea that the data searched was not private, in light of the nature and amount of information usually stored on cell phones and laptops.

Police at the door: Arrest warrants

If the police arrive at your home or office with an arrest warrant, go outside, lock the door, and give yourself up. Otherwise, they'll just force their way in and arrest you anyway, and then be able to search nearby. It is better to just go peacefully without giving them an excuse to search inside.

Police at the door: Searches of electronic devices incident to arrest

If you are arrested, the officers are going to seize all the property on your person before you are taken to jail. If you have a cell phone or a laptop, they will take that too. If you are sitting near a cell phone or laptop, they may take those as well. The SITA doctrine may allow police to search the data. It many also allow copying for later search, though this is well beyond what the SITA doctrine's original justification would allow.

You can and should password protect your devices to prevent this potentially unconstitutional privacy invasion. But for much stronger protection, consider protecting your data with file and disk encryption.

Prudent arresting officers will simply secure the devices while they get a warrant. There's nothing you can do to prevent that. Do not try to convince the officers to leave your phone or laptop behind by disavowing ownership. Lying to a police officer can be a crime. Also, prosecutors may use your statements against you later to argue that you do not have the right to challenge even an illegal search or seizure of the device, while still being able to introduce information stored on the device against you. Subpoenas.

Another Powerful Investigative Tool

In addition to search warrants, the government has another very powerful legal tool for getting evidence — the subpoena. Subpoenas are legal documents that demand that someone produce specific documents or appear in court to testify. The subpoena can be directed at you to produce evidence you have about yourself or someone else, or at a third party to produce evidence they have collected about you.

Subpoenas demand that you produce the requested evidence, or appear in court to testify, at some future time. Search warrants, on the other hand, are served and executed immediately by law enforcement with or without your cooperation.

Subpoenas, unlike search warrants, can be challenged in court before compliance. If you are the recipient of the subpoena, you can challenge it on the grounds that it is too broad or that it would be unduly burdensome to comply with it. If a judge agrees, then the court may quash the subpoena so you don't have to produce the requested evidence. You may also be able to quash the subpoena if it is seeking legally privileged material, or information that is protected by the First Amendment, such as a political organization's membership list or information to identify an anonymous speaker. If the subpoena is directed to a third party that holds information about you, and you find out about it before compliance, then you can make a motion to quash the subpoena on the grounds of privilege or constitutional rights regardless of whether the third party decides it would otherwise comply. However, you have to do so before the compliance date. Subpoenas that are used to get records about you from third parties sometimes require that you be notified, but usually do not.

Subpoenas are issued under a much lower standard than the probable cause standard used for search warrants. A subpoena can be used so long as there is any reasonable possibility that the materials or testimony sought will produce information relevant to the general subject of the investigation.

Subpoenas can be issued in civil or criminal cases and on behalf of government prosecutors or private litigants; often, subpoenas are merely signed by a government employee, a court clerk, or even a private attorney. In contrast, only the government can get a search warrant.

Police at the door: Subpoenas

What should you do if a government agent (or anyone else) shows up with a subpoena?

NOTHING.

Subpoenas are demands that you produce evidence at some time in the future. A subpoena does not give anyone the right to enter or search your home or office, nor does it require you to hand over anything immediately. Even a "subpoena forthwith", which asks for immediate compliance, can not be enforced without first going to a judge.

So, if someone shows up with a subpoena, don't answer any questions, don't invite them in, and don't consent to a search — just take the subpoena, say thank you, close the door and call a lawyer as soon as possible!

[This selection is part of a larger entry on Surveillance Self-Defense and can be found on the Electronic Frontier Foundation's SSD website at https://ssd.eff.org/]

NO SAFE QUARTER
LORELEY MACTAVISH

"If you're not doing anything wrong, you have nothing to worry about."

The above is a common phrase repeated often by the uninformed in regards to our growing surveillance society. Not only is it an uninformed opinion; it is irresponsible and unconscionable for those who call themselves Americans. *Those people,* as I've dubbed those who say such things, are effectively spitting upon the Constitution namely the Fourth Amendment.

Our society has disintegrated, becoming a place where everyone is considered a potential threat until proven innocent. But what is the definition of innocent? Innocent of what crime? Simply behaving "suspiciously" is now enough to be reported. For example, the Department of Homeland Security has launched the "If You See Something, Say Something" campaign. If you see *what?* The videos give examples of people leaving bags in public places. What about those of us who forget our items?

I've lost my purse, but I'd rather someone try to return it to me instead of calling the authorities!

One has to also wonder if holding political opinions is wrong. I always considered holding informed opinions as being responsible. However, in Pennsylvania, this was not considered as such. In fact, in the fall of 2010, watch lists were made of various groups – Tea Parties, anti-gas drillers, anti-puppy mill groups, etc. From this I gathered that being informed and having an opinion was considered threatening by the government, warranting attention from authorities!

For a long time after this, I was afraid to speak out and let my opinion be known, something I'd always enjoyed until then. Following the watch list incident, I'd have nightmares of DHS personnel hiding in the shrubbery, tapping my phones, listening to my conversations about underwear shopping or family problems. Sometimes I still do. When the lists were discovered, it was fear like I'd never known before. I felt betrayed, like all I'd believed about America was a lie, like some child finding out Santa Claus wasn't real. But this was worse. Knowing there's no fat man dressed in red to bring presents doesn't cause any sort of raw terror. Finding out the document I thought protected my rights was about as real as Narnia was quite another story.

Afterward, I spoke with many senior citizens who attended political events. (My old city had a large elderly population.) These folks in their walkers or toting canes were just as afraid as I, wondering if they would be barred from boarding a plane, wondering if there would be any repercussions to the lists.

Fear is, perhaps, one of the most powerful weapons to use against people. I still have bad dreams about those lists. And I didn't think I was doing anything wrong. I suppose since 9/11 that the definition of "wrong" has changed.

"If you have nothing to hide, you have nothing to worry about."

This is another rephrasing of the first quote, yet a little more insidious, a little farther reaching, if you will. Doing wrong and having nothing to hide can be two completely different things. This phrase suggests that you should be an open book. It also makes me think of that quote from Eric Schmidt of Google notoriety: "If you have something that you don't want anyone to know, maybe you shouldn't be doing it in the first place."[1]

How about going to rehab, marriage counseling, cancer treatment, purchasing scandalous lingerie, or treating an embarrassing health problem? It seems as if, according to Schmidt and *those people,* we all ought to ignore our personal problems, pretend they don't exist, wear "granny panties," and just let whatever that nasty little problem is continue untreated.

And, I for one, do have things to hide! Like my titties and hoo-hoo when I go to the airport. If I were a stripper, I'd have a lot more money. But, I certainly don't relish the thought of stripping for strangers for free. Oh, wait, actually, considering I buy the plane tickets, *I'm paying!* What kind of raw, pervy deal is that?

Going on vacation should not cause anxiety; it should be a fun, lighthearted time. Yet, waiting in the queue to be screened by those clunking around in jackboots tends to cause a large amount of anxiety. If you've ever been the victim of sexual harassment, the situation can be very bad, indeed. And then, of course, there's the thought that maybe I might have ended up on a list because someone in power didn't like a letter to the editor, a USPP newsletter, a speech I gave at a rally, or this essay. Now, I haven't done anything wrong, other than state my beliefs, a practice allegedly protected by the First Amendment.

It seems that people back in Pennsylvania forgot about that list. No one brings it up anymore. The head of the department stepped down after that fiasco and that seemed to satisfy the masses. Yet how can the people there feel they are safe to continue as they would? The Patriot Act is still in effect, the reason for the list in the first place.

It has frustrated me that no one seems to realize all the other issues don't matter if your voice is taken away. How can you speak if you'll be punished, watched like a criminal? If we allow our voice to be outlawed, we will have no say in anything.

To make it worse, the TSA is now moving to the streets in Tennessee. They set up checkpoints along roads! How long until this comes to other states? How long until we start getting questioned about personal effects in our vehicles and are forced to "show our papers?" How long until the biggest stressor while driving is no longer the harried person cutting off other motorists?

Perhaps one of the most disturbing items I've read about lately is IntelliStreets. These are streetlights that have the capability to take pictures, give security alerts, reprimand people for littering or jaywalking, and broadcast ads and security alerts. Yet, there's one other capability these devices have – the ability to record conversations!

Ron Harwood, the inventor of Intellistreets, claims, "This is not a system with spook technology."[2] Really? Then what is the purpose of street lights being able to record a conversation?

No Safe Harbor

Obviously there's a reason he decided to include that capability in his design, and I'm doubting it's because he's a voyeur.

How many freedoms have we lost? We're treated like criminals, have to fear expressing ourselves, must wonder if our phone conversations are being recorded…and the list goes on. However, far more than anything else, our own government and the corporations that benefit by creating this spook technology, to use Harwood's term, are what frighten me the most. Who is going to protect us from them?

THE UNIVERSAL DECLARATION FOR HUMAN RIGHTS
THE UNITED NATIONS

PREAMBLE

Whereas recognition of the inherent dignity and of the equal and inalienable rights of all members of the human family is the foundation of freedom, justice and peace in the world,

Whereas disregard and contempt for human rights have resulted in barbarous acts which have outraged the conscience of mankind, and the advent of a world in which human beings shall enjoy freedom of speech and belief and freedom from fear and want has been proclaimed as the highest aspiration of the common people,

Whereas it is essential, if man is not to be compelled to have recourse, as a last resort, to rebellion against tyranny and oppression, that human rights should be protected by the rule of law,

Whereas it is essential to promote the development of friendly relations between nations,

Whereas the peoples of the United Nations have in the Charter reaffirmed their faith in fundamental human rights, in the dignity and worth of the human person and in the equal rights of men and women and have determined to promote social progress and better standards of life in larger freedom,

Whereas Member States have pledged themselves to achieve, in co-operation with the United Nations, the promotion of universal respect for and observance of human rights and fundamental freedoms,

Whereas a common understanding of these rights and freedoms is of the greatest importance for the full realization of this pledge,

Now, Therefore THE GENERAL ASSEMBLY proclaims THIS UNIVERSAL DECLARATION OF HUMAN RIGHTS as a common standard of achievement for all peoples and all nations, to the end that every individual and every organ of society, keeping this Declaration constantly in mind, shall strive by teaching and education to promote respect for these rights and freedoms and by progressive measures, national and international, to secure their universal and effective recognition and observance, both among the peoples of Member States themselves and among the peoples of territories under their jurisdiction.

Article 1.

All human beings are born free and equal in dignity and rights. They are endowed with reason and conscience and should act towards one another in a spirit of brotherhood.

Article 2.

Everyone is entitled to all the rights and freedoms set forth in this Declaration, without distinction of any kind, such as race, color, sex, language, religion, political or other opinion, national or social origin, property, birth or other status. Furthermore, no distinction shall be made on the basis of the political, jurisdictional or international status of the country or territory to which a person belongs, whether it be independent, trust, non-self-governing or under any other limitation of sovereignty.

Article 3.

Everyone has the right to life, liberty and security of person.

Article 4.

No one shall be held in slavery or servitude; slavery and the slave trade shall be prohibited in all their forms.

Article 5.

No one shall be subjected to torture or to cruel, inhuman or degrading treatment or punishment.

Article 6.

Everyone has the right to recognition everywhere as a person before the law.

Article 7.

All are equal before the law and are entitled without any discrimination to equal protection of the law. All are entitled to equal protection against any discrimination in violation of this Declaration and against any incitement to such discrimination.

Article 8.

Everyone has the right to an effective remedy by the competent national tribunals for acts violating the fundamental rights granted him by the constitution or by law.

Article 9.

No one shall be subjected to arbitrary arrest, detention or exile.

Article 10.

Everyone is entitled in full equality to a fair and public hearing by an independent and impartial tribunal, in the determination of his rights and obligations and of any criminal charge against him.

Article 11.

(1). Everyone charged with a penal offense has the right to be presumed innocent until proved guilty according to law in a public trial at which he has had all the guarantees necessary for his defense.

(2). No one shall be held guilty of any penal offense on account of any act or omission which did not constitute a penal offense, under national or international law, at the time when it was committed. Nor shall a heavier penalty be imposed than the one that was applicable at the time the penal offense was committed.

Article 12.

No one shall be subjected to arbitrary interference with his privacy, family, home or correspondence, nor to attacks upon his honor and reputation. Everyone has the right to the protection of the law against such interference or attacks.

Article 13.

(1). Everyone has the right to freedom of movement and residence within the borders of each state.

(2). Everyone has the right to leave any country, including his own, and to return to his country.

Article 14.

(1). Everyone has the right to seek and to enjoy in other countries asylum from persecution.

(2). This right may not be invoked in the case of prosecutions genuinely arising from non-political crimes or from acts contrary to the purposes and principles of the United Nations.

Article 15.

(1). Everyone has the right to a nationality.

(2). No one shall be arbitrarily deprived of his nationality nor denied the right to change his nationality.

Article 16.

(1). Men and women of full age, without any limitation due to race, nationality or religion, have the right to marry and to found a family.

(2).They are entitled to equal rights as to marriage, during marriage and at its dissolution. Marriage shall be entered into only with the free and full consent of the intending spouses.

(3).The family is the natural and fundamental group unit of society and is entitled to protection by society and the State.

Article 17.

(1). Everyone has the right to own property alone as well as in association with others.

(2). No one shall be arbitrarily deprived of his property.

Article 18.

Everyone has the right to freedom of thought, conscience and religion; this right includes freedom to change his religion or belief, and freedom, either alone or in community with others and in public or private, to manifest his religion or belief in teaching, practice, worship and observance.

Article 19.

Everyone has the right to freedom of opinion and expression; this right includes freedom to hold opinions without interference and to seek, receive and impart information and ideas through any media and regardless of frontiers.

Article 20.

(1). Everyone has the right to freedom of peaceful assembly and association.

(2). No one may be compelled to belong to an association.

Article 21.

(1). Everyone has the right to take part in the government of his country, directly or through freely chosen representatives.

(2). Everyone has the right of equal access to public service in his country.

(3). The will of the people shall be the basis of the authority of government; this will shall be expressed in periodic and genuine elections which shall be by universal and equal suffrage and shall be held by secret vote or by equivalent free voting procedures.

Article 22.

Everyone, as a member of society, has the right to social security and is entitled to realization, through national effort and international co-operation and in accordance with the organization and resources of each State, of the economic, social and cultural rights indispensable for his dignity and the free development of his personality.

Article 23.

(1). Everyone has the right to work, to free choice of employment, to just and favorable conditions of work and to protection against unemployment.

(2). Everyone, without any discrimination, has the right to equal pay for equal work.

(3). Everyone who works has the right to just and favorable remuneration ensuring for himself and his family an existence worthy of human dignity, and supplemented, if necessary, by other means of social protection.

(4). Everyone has the right to form and to join trade unions for the protection of his interests.

Article 24.

Everyone has the right to rest and leisure, including reasonable limitation of working hours and periodic holidays with pay.

Article 25.

(1). Everyone has the right to a standard of living adequate for the health and well-being of himself and of his family, including food, clothing, housing and medical care and necessary social services, and the right to security in the event of unemployment, sickness, disability, widowhood, old age or other lack of livelihood in circumstances beyond his control.

(2). Motherhood and childhood are entitled to special care and assistance. All children, whether born in or out of wedlock, shall enjoy the same social protection.

Article 26.

(1). Everyone has the right to education. Education shall be free, at least in the elementary and fundamental stages. Elementary education shall be compulsory. Technical and professional education shall be made generally available and higher education shall be equally accessible to all on the basis of merit.

(2). Education shall be directed to the full development of the human personality and to the strengthening of respect for human rights and fundamental freedoms. It shall promote understanding, tolerance and friendship among all nations, racial or religious groups, and shall further the activities of the United Nations for the maintenance of peace.

(3). Parents have a prior right to choose the kind of education that shall be given to their children.

Article 27.

(1). Everyone has the right freely to participate in the cultural life of the community, to enjoy the arts and to share in scientific advancement and its benefits.

(2). Everyone has the right to the protection of the moral and material interests resulting from any scientific, literary or artistic production of which he is the author.

Article 28.

Everyone is entitled to a social and international order in which the rights and freedoms set forth in this Declaration can be fully realized.

Article 29.

(1). Everyone has duties to the community in which alone the free and full development of his personality is possible.

(2). In the exercise of his rights and freedoms, everyone shall be subject only to such limitations as are determined by law solely for the purpose of securing due recognition and respect for the rights and freedoms of others and of meeting the just requirements of morality, public order and the general welfare in a democratic society.

(3). These rights and freedoms may in no case be exercised contrary to the purposes and principles of the United Nations.

Article 30.

Nothing in this Declaration may be interpreted as implying for any State, group or person any right to engage in any activity or to perform any act aimed at the destruction of any of the rights and freedoms set forth herein.

[The Universal Declaration of Human Rights, which was adopted by the UN General Assembly on 10 December 1948, was the result of the experience of the Second World War. With the end of that war, and the creation of the United Nations, the international community vowed never again to allow atrocities like those of that conflict happen again. It can be found online at http://www.un.org/en/documents/udhr/index.shtml.]

No Safe Harbor

INTELLECTUAL PROPERTY

HISTORY OF COPYRIGHT
RICK FALKVINGE

In this essay, I will look at the history of copyright from 1350 until present day. The story of the history books differs quite strongly from what you usually hear from the copyright industry.

We're starting with the advent of the Black Death in Western Europe in the 1350s. Like all other places, Europe was hit hard: people fled westward from the Byzantine Empire and brought with them both the plague and scientific writings. It would take Europe 150 years to recover politically, economically, and socially.

The religious institutions were the ones to recover the slowest. Not only were they hit hard because of the dense congregation of monks and nuns, but they were also the last to be repopulated, as parents needed every available child in the family's economy, agriculture, et cetera, in the decades following the Plague.

This is relevant because monks and nuns were the ones making books in this time. When you wanted a book copied, you would go to a scribe at a monastery, and they would copy it for you. By hand. No copy would be perfect; every scribe would fix spelling and grammatical errors while making the copy, as well as introduce some new ones.

Also, since all scribes were employed (read controlled) by the Catholic Church, there was quite some limitation to what books would be produced. Not only was the monetary cost of a single book astronomical — one copy of The Bible required 170 calfskins or 300 sheepskins (!!) — but there was also a limit to what teachings would be reproduced by a person of the clergy. Nothing contradicting the Vatican was even remotely conceivable.

By 1450, the monasteries were still not repopulated, and the major cost of having a book copied was the services of the scribe, an under-supplied craft still in high demand. This puts things in proportion, given the astronomical cost of the raw materials and that they were a minor cost in ordering a book. In 1451, Gutenberg perfected the combination of the squeeze press, metal movable type, oil based print inks and block printing. At the same time, a new type of paper had been copied from the Chinese, a paper which was cheap to make and plentiful. This made scribecraft obsolete more or less overnight.

The printing press revolutionized society by creating the ability to spread information cheaply, quickly, and accurately.

The Catholic Church, which had previously controlled all information (and particularly held a cornered market on the scarcity of information), went on a rampage. They could no longer control what information would be reproduced, could no longer control what people knew, and lobbied kings across Europe for a ban on this technology which wrestled control of the populace from them.

Many arguments were used to justify this effort, trying to win the hearts of the people for going back to the old order. One notable argument was, "How will the monks get paid?"

The Catholic Church would eventually fail in this endeavor, paving the way for the Renaissance and the Protestant movement, but not before much blood had been spilled in trying to prevent the accurate, cheap and quick distribution of ideas, knowledge, and culture.

This attempt culminated in France on January 13, 1535, when a law was enacted at the request of the Catholic Church, a law which forced the closure of all bookshops and stipulated death penalty by hanging for anybody using a printing press.

This law was utterly ineffective. Pirate print shops lined the country's borders like a pearl necklace and pirate literature poured into France through contraband distribution channels built by ordinary people hungry for more things to read.

On May 23, 1533, Mary was formally declared a bastard by the archbishop. Her mother, Catherine, who was a catholic and the Pope's protegé, had been thrown out of the family by her father Henry, who had turned protestant just to get rid of Catherine. This was an injustice Mary would attempt to correct all her life.

King Henry VIII wanted a son to inherit the Throne of England for the Tudor dynasty, but his marriage was a disappointment. His wife, Catherine of Aragon, had only borne him a daughter, Mary. Worse still, the Pope would not let him divorce Catherine in the hope of finding someone else to bear him a son.

Henry's solution was quite drastic, effective, and novel. He converted all of England into Protestantism, founding the Church of England, in order to deny the Pope any influence over his marriage. Henry then had his marriage with Catherine of Aragon declared void on May 23, 1533, after which he went on to marry several other women in sequence. He had a second daughter with his second wife, and finally a son with his third wife. Unlike the bastard child Mary, her younger half-siblings — Elizabeth and Edward — were protestants.

Edward succeeded Henry VIII on the throne in 1547, at the age of nine. He died before reaching adult age. Mary was next in the line of succession, despite having been declared a bastard. Thus, the outcast ascended to the Throne of England with a vengeance as Mary I in 1553.

She had not spoken to her father for years and years. Rather, hers was the mission to undo her father's wrongdoings to the Faith, to England, and to her mother, and to turn England back into Catholicism. She persecuted protestants relentlessly, publicly executing several hundred, earning her the nickname Bloody Mary.

She shared the concern of the Catholic Church over the printing press. The public's ability to quickly distribute information en masse was dangerous to her ambitions to restore Catholicism, in particular their ability to distribute heretic material. (Political material, in this day and age, was not distinguishable from religious material.) Seeing how France had failed miserably in banning the printing press, even under threat of hanging, she realized another solution was needed. One that involved the printing industry in a way that would benefit them as well.

She devised a monopoly where the London printing guild would get a complete monopoly on all printing in England, in exchange for her censors determining what was fit to print beforehand. It was a very lucrative monopoly for the guild, who would be working hard to maintain the monopoly and the favor of the Queen's censors. This merger of corporate and governmental powers turned out to be effective in suppressing free speech and political-religious dissent.

The monopoly was awarded to the London Company of Stationers on May 4, 1557. It was called copyright.

It was widely successful as a censorship instrument. Working with the industry to suppress free speech worked, in contrast to the French attempt in the earlier 1500s to ban all printing by decree. The Stationers worked as a private censorship bureau, burning unlicensed books, impounding or destroying monopoly-infringing printing presses, and denying politically unsuitable material the light of day. Only in doubtful cases did they care to consult the Queen's censors for advice on what was allowed and what was not. Mostly, it was quite apparent after a few initial consultations.[4]

There was obviously a lust for reading, and the monopoly was very lucrative for the Stationers. As long as nothing politically destabilizing was in circulation, the common people were allowed their entertainment. It was a win-win for the repressive Queen and for the Stationers with a lucrative monopoly on their hands.

Mary I died just one year later, on November 17, 1558. She was succeeded by her protestant half-sister Elizabeth, who went on to become Elizabeth I and one of the highest-regarded regents of England ever. Mary's attempts to restore Catholicism to England had failed. Her invention of copyright, however, survives to this day.

After Bloody Mary had enacted the copyright censorship monopoly in 1557, neither the profitable industry guild nor the censoring Crown had any desire to abolish it. It would stand uninterrupted for 138 years.

As we have seen, the copyright monopoly was instituted as a censorship mechanism by Mary I in 1557 to prevent people from discussing or disseminating Protestant material. Her successor, Elizabeth I, was just as happy to keep the monopoly after Mary's death in 1558 to prevent people from discussing or disseminating Catholic material.

During the 1600s, Parliament gradually tried to wrestle control of the censorship from the Crown. In 1641, Parliament abolished the court where copyright cases had been tried, the infamous Star Chamber. In effect, this turned violation of the monopoly into a sentence-less crime, much like jaywalking in Sweden today: While it was still technically a crime, and technically illegal, you could not be tried for it and there was no punishment. As a result, creativity in Britain soared into the stratosphere.

Unfortunately, this wasn't what Parliament had had in mind at all.

In 1643, the copyright censorship monopoly was re-instituted with a vengeance. It included demands for pre-registrations of author, printer and publisher with the London Company of Stationers, a requirement for publication license before publishing anything, the right for the Stationers to impound, burn and destroy unlicensed equipment and books, and arrests and harsh punishments for anybody violating the copyright censorship.

Fast forwarding a bit, there was something called the Glorious Revolution in 1688, and Parliament's composition changed radically to mostly people who had previously been at the business end of censorship and weren't all too keen for that to continue. Therefore, the Stationers' monopoly was made to expire in 1695.

So from 1695 onward, there was no copyright. None. Creativity soared — again — and historians claim that many of the documents that eventually led to the founding of the United States of America were written in this time.

Unfortunately, the London Company of Stationers were not happy at all with the new order where they had lost their lucrative monopoly. They gathered their families on the stairs of Parliament and begged for the monopoly to be reinstated.

It is noteworthy that authors did not ask for the copyright monopoly: the printers and distributors did. There was never an argument along the lines that nothing would be written without copyright; the argument was that nothing would be printed without copyright. This is something else entirely.

Parliament, having just abolished censorship, was keen on not re-instituting a central point of control with a possible abuse potential. The Stationers' responded by suggesting that writers should "own" their works. In doing so, they killed three birds with one stone. One, Parliament would be assured that there was no central point of control which could be used to censor. Two, the publishers would retain a monopoly for all intents and purposes, as the writers would have nobody to sell their works to but the publishing industry. Three, and perhaps most importantly, the monopoly would be legally classified as Anglo-Saxon Common Law rather than the weaker Case Law, and therefore given much stronger legal protection.

The publishing lobby got as they wanted, and the new copyright monopoly was re-enacted in 1709, taking effect on April 10, 1710. This was the copyright lobby's first major victory.

What we see at this point in history is copyright in its unspun form: a monopoly with heritage from censorship where artists and authors were not even considered, but where it was always for the publishers' profit.

Also, the Stationers would continue to impound, destroy and burn others' printing presses for a long time, despite not having the right any longer. Abuse of power came immediately, and would last until the pivotal Entick vs. Carrington case in 1765, when yet another of these raids for "unlicensed" (read unwanted) authors had taken place. In the verdict of this court case in 1765, it was firmly established that no right may be denied to any citizen if not expressly forbidden by law, and that no authority may take itself any right not explicitly given by law.

Thus, the very first foundations of modern democracy and civil liberties were won in the battle against the copyright monopoly. There is nothing new under the sun.

United States Pirate Party

When the United States was founded, the concept of monopolies on ideas was carried to the New World and debated intensely. Thomas Jefferson was a fierce opponent to the monster of monopolies on ideas. A compromise was reached.

Copyright didn't originate in the United States, as we have seen. The idea had been there beforehand and the Founding Fathers carried the laws with them into their new country. The topic of monopolies on ideas, however, was a topic not easily settled. Jefferson wrote:

> If nature has made any one thing less susceptible than all others of exclusive property, it is the action of the thinking power called an idea, which an individual may exclusively possess as long as he keeps it to himself; but the moment it is divulged, it forces itself into the possession of every one, and the receiver cannot dispossess himself of it. Its peculiar character, too, is that no one possesses the less, because every other possesses the whole of it. He who receives an idea from me, receives instruction himself without lessening mine; as he who lights his taper at mine, receives light without darkening me. That ideas should freely spread from one to another over the globe, for the moral and mutual instruction of man, and improvement of his condition, seems to have been peculiarly and benevolently designed by nature, when she made them … incapable of confinement or exclusive appropriation.

In the end, the United States Constitution was the first one to specify the **reason** for copyrights (and patents!) to be granted. It is very clear and straightforward in its justification for the existence of copyright in United States law:

…to promote the progress of the sciences and useful arts…

It is particularly notable that the purpose of the monopoly was not for any profession to make money, neither writer nor printer nor distributor. Instead, the purpose is exemplary in its clarity: the only justification for the monopoly is if it **maximizes the culture and knowledge available to society**.

Thus, copyright (in the US, and therefore predominantly today) **is a balance between the public's access to culture and the same public's interest of having new culture created. This** is tremendously important. In particular, note here that **the public is the only legitimate stakeholder** in the wording and evolution of copyright law: the monopoly holders, while certainly being benefactors of the monopoly, are not legitimate stakeholders and should have no say in its wording, just like a regiment town should have no say in whether that regiment is actually needed for national security.

It is useful to point at the wording of the US Constitution when people falsely believe that the copyright monopoly exists so that artists can make money. It never did, not in any country.

Meanwhile in the United Kingdom

In the meantime in the United Kingdom, books were still quite expensive, mostly because of the copyright monopoly. Book collections were only seen in rich men's homes, and some started benevolently to lend books to the common people.

The publishers went mad about this, and lobbied Parliament to outlaw the reading of a book without first paying for their own copy. They tried to outlaw the public library before the library had even been invented. "Reading without paying first? That's stealing from the authors! Taking the bread right out of their childrens' mouths!"

But Parliament took a different stance, seeing the positive impact of reading on society. The problem perceived by Parliament was not the self-described eternal plight of the copyright monopolists, but the problem that rich men in society dictated who would read and who wouldn't. It seemed beneficial to society to level the playing field: to create public libraries, accessible to poor and rich alike.

The copyright monopolists went absolutely ballistic when they heard about this idea. "You can't let anybody read any book for free! Not a single book will be sold ever again! Nobody will be able to live off their writing! No author will write a single book ever again if you pass this law!"

Parliament in the 1800s was much wiser than today, however, and saw the copyright monopolists' tantrum for what it was. Parliament took a strong stance that public access to knowledge and culture had a larger benefit to society than the copyright monopoly, and so in 1849, the law instituting public libraries in the UK was passed. The first public library opened in 1850.

And as we know, not a single book has been written ever since. Either that, or the copyright monopolists' rant about nothing being created without a strong monopoly was as false then as it is when repeated today.

(Note: in some European countries, authors and translators get some pennies for every book lent from a library. It should be strongly noted that this is not a compensation for an imaginary loss of income, as if every reduction in the monopoly required compensation, but a national cultural grant which happens to measure popularity and therefore suitability for that grant using statistics from libraries. Besides, the grant appeared in the early 1900s, long after libraries.)

Meanwhile in Germany

Germany had no copyright monopoly during this time. Several historians argue that this led to the rapid proliferation of knowledge that enabled Germany to take the industrial lead over the United Kingdom — knowledge could be spread cheaply and efficiently. So in a way, Germany's leapfrogging of the United Kingdom proved British Parliament right: the national interest of access to culture and knowledge does supersede the monopoly interest of the publishers.

In the late 1800s, the publishers' ever-strengthening copyright monopoly had lopsided the creators' chances of making any revenue off of their works. Basically, all the money went to publishers and distributors, and creators were left starving, due to the copyright monopoly. (Just like today.)

A person in France named Victor Hugo would take the initiative to try to level the playing field by internationalizing a French tradition known as *droit d'auteur*, "writer's right," into the copyright monopoly. Also, he would try to make the copyright monopoly international: until now, it had just been a national monopoly. A French writer could sell his monopoly to a French publisher, and the publisher would enjoy monopoly powers in France, but not in Germany or the United Kingdom. Hugo sought to change this.

Paradoxically, the copyright and patent monopolies were forgotten when free market laws were enacted across Europe in the mid-1800s. Patent law still talks about "prevention of disloyal competition" as justification for its existence, which is a remnant from when guilds dictated products, craftsmen, and prices; if a business practices loyal competition in their industry segment today, we raid them at dawn and haul their ass to court. The copyright monopoly is a similar remnant from the printing guild of London.

Victor Hugo would try to balance the immense powers of the publishers by giving creators some rights under the copyright monopoly as well, unfortunately impoverishing the public further. (It is important here to remember that there are three parties to the copyright conflict: creators, publishers, and the public. Ironically, the public is the only legitimate stakeholder in the monopoly's design.)

While Hugo didn't live to see the fruition of his initiative, the Berne Convention was signed in 1886. It said that countries should respect the copyrights of other countries, and an agency — BIRPI — was set up as watchdog. This agency has mutated, grown and swelled and is today WIPO, which still oversees the Berne Convention, which has also swelled, mutated and been hijacked twice. (More on this shortly.)

So, at this point, there are four aspects of the copyright monopoly, which have more differences between them than similarities:

One, the **commercial monopoly to fixations of a work.** This is the original monopoly granted to London's printing guild in exchange for censorship.

Two, the **commercial monopoly to performances of a work.** If somebody performs a work publicly on a for-profit stage, the monopoly holder has a right to demand money.

Three, the **droit moral to be acknowledged as creator.** The right for an author or artist to be acknowledged as creator of his or her work, acting as protection against counterfeiting and against plagiarism.

Four, the **droit moral to veto an improper performance of the work.** If an artist feels that a performance slights the work or the name of the artist, they have the right to deny that performance the light of day.

The droits morals are very different in nature from the commercial monopolies in that they cannot be sold or transferred. This sets them sharply apart from the justification that convinced British Parliament to re-enact the copyright monopoly in 1709.

It is also noteworthy how often these four aspects are deliberately confused to defend the most controversial and damaging of the monopolies, the commercial monopoly on fixations (and later duplication). You will often hear people from the copyright industry defending the monopoly by asking "would you want somebody else to take your work and claim it was theirs?". However, this is the quite uncontroversial third part, the droit moral of attribution and credit, which cannot honestly be used to defend any of the two commercial monopolies.

The United States didn't like moral rights, by the way, so they stayed outside of the Berne Convention until they could use it for leverage against Toyota a hundred years later. We'll return to that soon.

During most of the 20th century, a battle of prominence raged between performing musicians and the record industry. For most of the century, musicians were regarded as the important party in law and in common sense. However, the record industry would rather see music corporativized. Active intervention by the self-declared fascist regime in Italy tipped the scales in this direction.

Copyright in the 20th century was not characterized by books, but by music. The 1930s saw two major developments that affected musicians: the Great Depression, which caused many musicians to lose their jobs, and movies with sound, which caused most of the rest of musicians to lose their jobs.

In this environment, two initiatives were taken in parallel. Musician's unions tried to guarantee income and sustenance to the people who were now jobless, made redundant as we say today in executive-speak. Unions all over the West were concerned about the spread of "mechanized music": any music that isn't performed live and therefore didn't need performing musicians. They wanted some power over the speaker technology, and the question was raised through the International Labour Organization (a predecessor to the UN agency with the same name).

At the same time, the record industry tried to exert the exact same power over speakers, radio and musicians. However, the entire political and business world at that time regarded them as a service contractor to the musicians. They could go about running their business if they were service-minded enough, or go bankrupt trying, and weren't worth diddlysquat more than that to anyone. Anyone, with just one exception:

Fascist Italy.

(This word, fascist, is loaded with emotion today. Italy's regime at this time were self-declared fascists. I'm using the word to describe them exactly as they described themselves.)

In 1933, the phonographic industry was invited to Rome by Confederazione Generale Fascista dell'Industria Italiana and under the protection of same. At this conference, held on November 10-14, an international federation of the phonographic industry was formed. It would later be more known under its acronym, IFPI. It was agreed that IFPI would try to work within the Berne Convention to establish producers' rights similar to those of the musicians and artists (which were always sold to publishers).

IFPI continued to meet in countries which welcomed their corporativist agenda, so they met in Italy the next year too, in Stresa. 1935 and onwards proved a bit turbulent for the world at large, but Italy still enacted thecorporativist rights of the record industry in 1937.

Negotiations for a copyright-like monopoly, attached to Berne and therefore international, was still too tempting for the record industry to resist. So after the war, IFPI reconvened in para-fascist Portugal in 1950. Italy wasn't suitable anymore, and the conference readied a draft text that would give them copyright-identical monopolies, so-called "neighboring rights," for producing and printing creative works such as music. This monopoly would be practically identical to the commercial copyright monopoly for fixations of a creative work.

The neighboring rights were ratified by BIRPI (today WIPO) **in 1961 in the so-called Rome Convention, giving the record**

industry copyright-identical monopolies. At the same time, ILO's attempt to give musicians similar rights had flopped, waned, and failed.

Since 1961, the record industry has feverishly defended copyright, despite the fact that it doesn't enjoy any copyright monopoly, only the copyright-identical monopoly known as "neighboring rights."

One needs to remember two things at this point:

First, the record industry is confusing all these monopolies on purpose. It keeps defending "its copyright," which it doesn't have, and talks nostalgically about how this copyright monopoly was created in great wisdom during the dawn of the Enlightenment [insert sunset and kittens here], referring to the Statute of Anne in 1709, which wasn't the first copyright anyway. In reality, the neighboring-rights monopolies were created in fascist countries (literally!) in a sunder-militarized recent Europe as late as 1961. These monopolies have been controversial and questioned from day one in 1961, and were certainly not the product of any Enlightenment wisdom.

Second, we were but a hair's breadth from still regarding the record labels as service bureaus for musicians, had ILO not failed, instead of the chokehold on musicians that they have been for the past decades. This would have been the case if it had not been for two intervening fascist governments — fascist in the literal sense of the word — supporting the record industry in corporativizing society and becoming the copyright industry.

Siege of the Middlemen

Throughout the 20th century, people involved with the copyright monopoly as middlemen rather than artists fought tooth and nail against every new development of technology and culture alike. The current claims against people sharing on the net should be seen in the light of this history.

United States Pirate Party

Earlier, we looked at how the record industry middlemen did a successful regulatory capture in putting themselves in the middle of the economy. As we learn from history, this has been the norm with the middlemen's behavior rather than the exception, but the last century has really seen this accelerate.

It started around 1905, when the self-playing piano was becoming popular. Sellers of note sheet music proclaimed that this would be the end of artistry if they couldn't make a living off of being middlemen between composers and the public, so they called for a ban on the player piano.

In the 1920s, as broadcast radio started appearing, another copyright industry was demanding its ban because it cut into profits. This time, it was the business of pay telephone numbers that played music over the phone. "If people can listen to music for free with this radio thing, artists will starve!" This argument was re-used through most of the century, with the word "radio" replaced by the most recent technology.

In the 1930s, silent movies were phased out by movies with audio tracks. Every theater had previously employed an orchestra that played music to accompany the silent movies, and now, these were out of a job. It is quite conceivable that this is the single worst technical development for professional performers. Their unions demanded guaranteed jobs for these performers in varying propositions.

In the 1960s, the copyright industry was fretting over people taping music off of radio, and tried to have the practice banned. The debate died off about the same time it was pointed out that this ban was technically impossible with anything less than installing cameras in people's living rooms.

The 1970s saw the advent of the cassette tape, which is when the copyright industry really went all-out in proclaiming their entitlement.

Ads saying "Home taping is killing music!" were everywhere. One band responded by subtly changing the message by changing "music" to "music industry," and "We left this side [of their tape] blank, so you can help." It saw many other parodies, too; regardless, the copyright industry were acting very seriously on the message.

The 1970s also saw another significant shift, where DJs started taking the place of live dance music. Musicians' unions and the copyright industry went ballistic over this, and suggested a "disco fee" that would be charged at locations playing disco (recorded) music, to be collected by private organizations under governmental mandate and redistributed to live bands. This produces a heartily laughter today, but that laughter stops sharp with the realization that the disco fee was actually introduced, and still exists.

The 1980s is a special chapter with the advent of video recording. The copyright industry's famous quote when testifying before the US Congress - where the film lobby's highest representative said that "The VCR is to the American film producer and the American public as the Boston strangler is to the woman home alone" -- is the stuff of legend today. Still, it bears reminding that the Betamax Case went all the way to the Supreme Court, and that the VCR was as near as could be to being killed by the copyright industry: The Betamax team won the case by 5-4 in votes at the United States Supreme Court.

Also in the late 1980s, we saw the complete flop of the Digital Audio Tape (DAT). A lot of this can be ascribed to the fact that the copyright industry had been allowed to put its politics into the design: The cassette, although technically superior to the analog Compact Cassette, was so deliberately unusable for copying music that people rejected it flat outright. This is an example of a technology that the copyright industry succeeded in killing, even though I doubt it was intentional: They just got their wishes as to how it should work to not disrupt the status quo.

United States Pirate Party

In 1994, the Fraunhofer Institute published a prototype implementation of its digital coding technique that would revolutionize digital audio. It allowed CD-quality audio to take one-tenth of the disk space, which was very valuable in this time, when a typical hard drive would be just a couple of gigabytes. Technically known as MPEG-1 Audio Layer III, it was quickly shortened to "MP3" in everyday speak. The copyright industry screamed again, calling it a technology that only can be used for criminal activity. The first successful MP3 player, the Diamond Rio, saw the light in 1998. It had 32 megabytes of memory. Despite good sales, the copyright industry sued its maker, Diamond Multimedia, into oblivion: While the lawsuit was eventually struck down, the company did not recover from the burden of defending. The monopoly middlemen tried aggressively to have MP3 players banned, just like every previous piece of new technology.

The century ended with the copyright middlemen pushing through a new law in the United States called the Digital Millennium Copyright Act. For the first time, the copyright industry managed to introduce intermediary liability -- as in making people liable in a court of law for merely carrying a signal which is broadcast by somebody else. Just like if you put up a public wall, and would become responsible for posters that other people put up on it: Not sane anywhere, but this isn't about sanity, it is about regulatory captures and enshrining the continued profit of monopolists into books of law.

The century also ended on a positive note, as Napster hit the light of day in 1999. Deservingly, the middlemen's handling of Napster is described as as a textbook example of an industry business failure in a delusion of entitlement.

In the final section, we'll take a look at how all the monopoly industries joined together to hold the entire economy for ransom.

Toyota struck at the heart of the American soul in the 1970s, and all her politicians started carrying mental "The End Is Nigh" signs. The most American things of all — cars! The American Cars! — weren't good enough for the American people. They all bought Toyota instead. This was an apocalypse-grade sign that United States was approaching its end as an industrial nation, unable to compete with Asia.

The period of 1960 to 2010 is marked by two things: one, the record-label-driven creepage of the copyright monopoly into the noncommercial, private domain where it was always a commercial-only monopoly before ("home taping is illegal" and such nonsense) and the monopoly therefore threatening fundamental human rights, and two, the corporate political expansion of the copyright monopoly and other monopolies.

When it was clear to politicians that the United States would no longer be able to maintain its economic dominance by producing anything industrially valuable or viable, many committees were formed and tasked with coming up with the answer to one crucial question: How can the US maintain its global dominance if (or when) it is not producing anything competitively valuable?

The response came from an unexpected direction: Pfizer.

The president of Pfizer, Edmund Pratt, had a furious op-ed piece in a New York Times on July 9, 1982 titled "Stealing from the Mind." It fumed about how third world countries were stealing from them. (By this, he referred to making medicine from their own raw materials with their own factories using their own knowledge in their own time for their own people, who were frequently dying from horrible but curable third-world conditions.) Major policymakers saw a glimpse of an answer in Pfizer's and Pratt's thinking, and turned to Pratt's involvement in another committee directly under the President. This committee was the magic ACTN: Advisory Committee on Trade Negotiations.

What the ACTN recommended, following Pfizer's lead, was so daring and provocative that nobody was really sure whether to try it out: The US would try linking its trade negotiations and foreign policy. Any country who didn't sign lopsided "free trade" deals that heavily redefined value would be branded in a myriad of bad ways, the most notable being the "Special 301 watchlist." This list is supposed to be a list of nations not respecting copyright enough. A majority of the world's population is on it, among them Canada.

So the solution to not producing anything of value in international trade was to redefine "producing," "anything," and "value" in an international political context, and to do so by bullying. It worked. The ACTN blueprints were set in motion by US Trade Representatives, using unilateral bullying to push foreign governments into enacting legislation that favored American industry interests, bilateral "free trade" agreements that did the same, and multilateral agreements that raised the bar worldwide in protection of American interests.

In this way, the United States was able to create an exchange of values where they would rent out blueprints and get finished products from those blueprints in return. This would be considered as a fair deal under the "free trade" agreements which redefined value artificially.

The entire US monopolized industry was behind this push: The copyright industries, the patent industries, all of them. They went forum shopping and tried to go to WIPO — repeating the hijack of the record industry in 1961 — to seek legitimacy and hostship for a new trade agreement that would be marketed as "Berne Plus".

At this point, it became politically necessary for the US to join the Berne Convention for credibility reasons, as WIPO is the overseer of Berne.

However, WIPO saw right through this scheme and more or less kicked them right out the door. WIPO was not created to give any country that kind of advantage over the rest of the world. They were outraged at the shameless attempt to hijack the copyright and patent monopolies.

So, another forum was needed. The US monopoly industry consortium approached GATT — the General Agreement on Tariffs and Trade — and managed to get influence there. A major process was initiated whereby about half of the participating countries in GATT were tricked, coerced or bullied into agreeing with a new agreement under GATT, an agreement which would lock in the Berne Convention and strengthen the US industry considerably on top of that by redefining "producing," "thing," and "value." This agreement was called TRIPs. Upon ratification of the TRIPs agreement, the GATT body was renamed WTO, the **World Trade Organization**. The 52 GATT countries choosing to stay out of the WTO would soon find themselves in an economic position where it became economically impossible to not sign the colonializing terms. Only one country out of the original 129 has not rejoined.

TRIPs has been under considerable fire for how it is constructed to enrich the rich at the expense of the poor, and when they can't pay with money, they pay with their health and sometimes their lives. It forbids third world countries from making medicine in their own factories from their own raw materials with their own knowledge to their own people. After several near-revolts, some concessions were made in TRIPs to "allow" for this.

But perhaps the most telling story of how important the artificial monopolies are to the United States' dominance came when Russia sought admission into the WTO (for incomprehensible reasons). To allow Russia admission, the United States demanded that the Russia-legal music shop AllofMP3 should be closed. This shop sold copies of

MP3 files and was classified as a radio station in Russia, paying appropriate license fees and was fully legal.

Now, let's go back a bit to review what was going on. This was the United States and Russia sitting at the negotiating table. Former enemies who kept each other at **nuclear gunpoint** 24 hours a day, 7 days a week, through sandstorm and blizzard. The United States could have demanded and gotten anything. Absolutely anything.

So what did the United States demand?

It asked for Russia to **close a bloody record store**.

That's when you realize how much there is to these monopolies.

To conclude:

File sharing is not just a private matter. It's a matter of global economic dominance, and always has been. Let's keep sharing and move that power from the monopolists to the people. Teach everybody to share culture, and the people will win against the constrainers of liberties, just as happened at the start of this essay, when people learned to read for themselves and toppled the Catholic Church.

(Lately, the copyright and patent industries have sought to repeat the TRIPs trick with ACTA, which they now call "Trips Plus." This is not finished yet as the last word hasn't been said.)

This concludes the history of the copyright monopoly as of 2011. Let's make sure we can write another chapter in ten years and are freer than ever to publish, share and spread it.

[This essay was originally published as a seven-part series on the author's website, http://falkvinge.net.]

THE DRM SAUSAGE FACTORY
CORY DOCTOROW

Otto von Bismarck quipped, "Laws are like sausages, it is better not to see them being made." I've seen sausages made. I've seen laws made. Both pale in comparison to the process by which anti-copying technology agreements are made.

This technology, usually called "Digital Rights Management" (DRM) proposes to make your computer worse at copying some of the files on its hard-drive or on other media. Since all computer operations involve copying, this is a daunting task -- as security expert Bruce Schneier has said, "Making bits harder to copy is like making water that's less wet."

At root, DRMs are technologies that treat the owner of a computer or other device as an attacker, someone against whom the system must be armored. Like the electrical meter on the side of your house, a DRM is a technology that you possess, but that you are never supposed to be able to manipulate or modify. Unlike your meter, though, a DRM that is defeated in one place is defeated in all places, nearly simultaneously. That is to say, once someone takes the DRM off a song or movie or ebook, that freed collection of bits can be sent to anyone else, anywhere the network reaches, in an eyeblink. DRM crackers need cunning: those who receive the fruits of their labor need only know how to download files from the Internet.

Why manufacture a device that attacks its owner? A priori, one would assume that such a device would cost more to make than a friendlier one, and that customers would prefer not to buy devices that treat them as presumptive criminals. DRM technologies limit more than copying: they limit ranges of uses, such as viewing a movie in a different country, copying a song to a different manufacturer's player, or even pausing a movie for too long. Surely, this stuff hurts sales: who goes into a store and asks, "Do you have any music that's locked to just one company's player? I'm in the market for some lock-in."

So why do manufacturers do it? As with many strange behaviors, there's a carrot at play here, and a stick.

The carrot is the entertainment industries' promise of access to their copyrighted works. Add DRM to your iPhone and we'll supply music for it. Add DRM to your TiVo and we'll let you plug it into our satellite receivers. Add DRM to your Zune and we'll let you retail our music in your Zune store.

The stick is the entertainment industries' threat of lawsuits for companies that don't comply. In the last century, entertainment companies fought over the creation of records, radios, jukeboxes, cable TV, VCRs, MP3 players and other technologies that made it possible to experience a copyrighted work in a new way without permission. There's one battle that serves as the archetype for the rest: the fight over the VCR.

The film studios were outraged by Sony's creation of the VCR. They had found a DRM supplier they preferred, a company called Discovision that made non-recordable optical discs. Discovision was the only company authorized to play back movies in your living room. The only way to get a copyrighted work onto a VCR cassette was to record it off the TV, without permission. The studios argued that Sony -- whose Betamax was the canary in this legal coalmine -- was breaking the law by unjustly endangering their revenue from Discovision royalties. Sure, they *could* just sell pre-recorded Betamax tapes, but Betamax was a read-write medium: they could be *copied*. Moreover, your personal library of Betamax recordings of the Sunday night movie would eat into the market for Discovision discs: why would anyone buy a pre-recorded video cassette when they could amass all the video they needed with a home recorder and a set of rabbit-ears?

The Supreme Court threw out these arguments in a 1984 5-4 decision, the "Betamax Decision." This decision held that the VCR was legal because it was "capable of sustaining a substantially non-infringing use." That means that if you make a technology that your customers *can* use legally, you're not on the hook for the illegal stuff they do.

This principle guided the creation of virtually every piece of IT invented since: the Web, search engines, YouTube, Blogger, Skype, ICQ, AOL, MySpace... You name it, if it's possible to violate copyright with it, the thing that made it possible is the Betamax principle.

Unfortunately, the Supremes shot the Betamax principle in the gut two years ago [ed: 2005], with the Grokster decision. This decision says that a company can be found liable for its customers' bad acts if they can be shown to have "induced" copyright infringement. So, if your company advertises your product for an infringing use, or if it can be shown that you had infringement in mind at the design stage, you can be found liable for your customers' copying. The studios and record labels and broadcasters *love* this ruling, and they like to think that it's even broader than what the courts set out. For example, Viacom is suing Google for inducing copyright infringement by allowing YouTube users to flag some of their videos as private. Private videos can't be found by Viacom's copyright-enforcement bots, so Viacom says that privacy should be illegal, and that companies that give you the option of privacy should be sued for anything you do behind closed doors.

The gutshot Betamax doctrine will bleed out all over the industry for decades (or until the courts or Congress restore it to health), providing a grisly reminder of what happens to companies that try to pour the entertainment companies' old wine into new digital bottles without permission. The tape-recorder was legal, but the digital tape-recorder is an inducement to infringement, and must be stopped.

The promise of access to content and the threat of legal execution for non-compliance is enough to lure technology's biggest players to the DRM table.

I started attending DRM meetings in March, 2002, on behalf of my former employers, the Electronic Frontier Foundation. My first meeting was the one where Broadcast Flag was born. The Broadcast Flag was weird even by DRM standards. Broadcasters are required, by law, to deliver TV and radio without DRM, so that any standards-compliant receiver can receive them. The airwaves belong to the public, and are loaned to broadcasters who have to promise to serve the public interest in exchange. But the MPAA and the broadcasters wanted to add DRM to digital TV, and so they proposed that a law should be passed that would make all manufacturers promise to *pretend* that there was DRM on broadcast signals, receiving them and immediately squirreling them away in encrypted form.

The Broadcast Flag was hammered out in a group called the Broadcast Protection Discussion Group (BPDG) a sub-group from the MPAA's "Content Protection Technology Working Group," which also included reps from all the big IT companies (Microsoft, Apple, Intel, and so on), consumer electronics companies (Panasonic, Philips, Zenith), cable companies, satellite companies, and anyone else who wanted to pay $100 to attend the "public" meetings, held every six weeks or so (you can attend these meetings yourself if you find yourself near LAX on one of the upcoming dates).

CPTWG (pronounced Cee-Pee-Twig) is a venerable presence in the DRM world. It was at CPTWG that the DRM for DVDs was hammered out. CPTWG meetings open with a "benediction," delivered by a lawyer, who reminds everyone there that what they say might be quoted "on the front page of the New York Times," (though journalists are barred from attending CPTWG meetings and no minutes are published by the organization) and reminding all present not to do anything that would raise eyebrows at the FTC's anti-trust division (I could swear I've seen the Microsoft people giggling during this part, though that may have been my imagination).

The first part of the meeting is usually taken up with administrative business and presentations from DRM vendors, who come out to promise that this time they've really, really figured out how to make computers worse at copying. The real meat comes after the lunch, when the group splits into a series of smaller meetings, many of them closed-door and private (the representatives of the organizations responsible for managing DRM on DVDs splinter off at this point).

Then comes the working group meetings, like the BPDG. The BPDG was nominally set up to set up the rules for the Broadcast Flag. Under the Flag, manufacturers would be required to limit their "outputs and recording methods" to a set of "approved technologies." Naturally, every manufacturer in the room showed up with a technology to add to the list of approved technologies -- and the sneakier ones showed up with reasons why their competitors' technologies *shouldn't* be approved. If the Broadcast Flag became law, a spot on the "approved technologies" list would be a license to print money: everyone who built a next-gen digital TV would be required, by law, to buy only approved technologies for their gear.

The CPTWG determined that there would be three "chairmen" of the meetings: A representative from the broadcasters, a representative from the studios, and a representative from the IT industry (note that no "consumer rights" chair was contemplated -- we proposed one and got laughed off the agenda). The IT chair was filled by an Intel representative, who seemed pleased that the MPAA chair, Fox Studios' Andy Setos, began the process by proposing that the approved technologies should include only two technologies, both of which Intel partially owned.

Intel's presence on the committee was both reassurance and threat: reassurance because Intel signaled the fundamental reasonableness of the MPAA's requirements -- why would a company with a bigger turnover than the whole movie industry show up if the negotiations weren't worth having? Threat because Intel was poised to gain an advantage that might be denied to its competitors.

We settled in for a long negotiation. The discussions were drawn out and heated. At regular intervals, the MPAA reps told us that we were wasting time -- if we didn't hurry things along, the world would move on and consumers would grow accustomed to un-crippled digital TVs. Moreover, Rep Billy Tauzin, the lawmaker who'd evidently promised to enact the Broadcast Flag into law, was growing impatient. The warnings were delivered in quackspeak, urgent and crackling, whenever the discussions dragged, like the crack of the commissars' pistols, urging us forward.

You'd think that a "technology working group" would concern itself with technology, but there was precious little discussion of bits and bytes, ciphers and keys. Instead, we focused on what amounted to contractual terms: If your technology got approved as a DTV "output," what obligations would you have to assume? If a TiVo could serve as an "output" for a receiver, what outputs would the TiVo be allowed to have?

The longer we sat there, the more snarled these contractual terms became: Winning a coveted spot on the "approved technology" list would be quite a burden! Once you were in the club, there were all sorts of rules about whom you could associate with, how you had to comport yourself and so on.

One of these rules of conduct was "robustness." As a condition of approval, manufacturers would have to harden their technologies so that their customers wouldn't be able to modify, improve upon, or even understand their workings. As you might imagine, the people who made open source TV tuners were not thrilled about this, as "open source" and "non-user-modifiable" are polar opposites.

Another was "renewability:" the ability of the studios to revoke outputs that had been compromised in the field. The studios expected the manufacturers to make products with remote "kill switches" that could be used to shut down part or all of their device if someone, somewhere had figured out how to do something naughty with it. They promised that we'd establish criteria for renewability later, and that it would all be "fair."

But we soldiered on. The MPAA had a gift for resolving the worst snarls: When shouting failed, they'd lead any recalcitrant player out of the room and negotiate in secret with them, leaving the rest of us to cool our heels. Once, they took the Microsoft team out of the room for *six hours*, then came back and announced that digital video would be allowed to output on non-DRM monitors at a greatly reduced resolution (this "feature" appears in Vista as "fuzzing").

The further we went, the more nervous everyone became. We were headed for the real meat of the negotiations: The *criteria* by which approved technology would be evaluated: How many bits of crypto would you need? Which ciphers would be permissible? Which features would and wouldn't be allowed?

Then the MPAA dropped the other shoe: The sole criteria for inclusion on the list would be the approval of one of its member-companies, or a quorum of broadcasters. In other words, the Broadcast

Flag wouldn't be an "objective standard," describing the technical means by which video would be locked away -- it would be purely subjective, up to the whim of the studios. You could have the best product in the world, and they wouldn't approve it if your business-development guys hadn't bought enough drinks for their business-development guys at a CES party.

To add insult to injury, the only technologies that the MPAA were willing to consider for initial inclusion as "approved" were the two that Intel was involved with. The Intel co-chairman had a hard time hiding his grin. He'd acted as Judas goat, luring in Apple, Microsoft, and the rest, to legitimize a process that would force them to license Intel's patents for every TV technology they shipped until the end of time.

Why did the MPAA give Intel such a sweetheart deal? At the time, I figured that this was just straight quid pro quo, like Hannibal said to Clarice. But over the years, I started to see a larger pattern: Hollywood likes DRM consortia, and they hate individual DRM vendors. (I've written an entire article about this, but here's the gist: A single vendor who succeeds can name their price and terms -- think of Apple or Macrovision -- while a consortium is a more easily divided rabble, susceptible to co-option in order to produce ever-worsening technologies -- think of Blu-Ray and HD-DVD). Intel's technologies were held through two consortia, the 5C and 4C groups.

The single-vendor manufacturers were livid at being locked out of the digital TV market. The final report of the consortium reflected this -- a few sheets written by the chairmen describing the "consensus" and hundreds of pages of angry invective from manufacturers and consumer groups decrying it as a sham.

Tauzin washed his hands of the process: A canny, sleazy Hill operator, he had the political instincts to get his name off any proposal that could be shown to be a plot to break voters' televisions (Tauzin found a better industry to shill for, the pharmaceutical firms, who rewarded him with a $2,000,000/year job as chief of PHARMA, the pharmaceutical lobby).

Even Representative Ernest "Fritz" Hollings ("The Senator from Disney," who once proposed a bill requiring entertainment industry oversight of all technologies capable of copying) backed away from proposing a bill that would turn the Broadcast Flag into law. Instead, Hollings sent a memo to Michael Powell, then-head of the FCC, telling him that the FCC already had jurisdiction to enact a Broadcast Flag regulation, without Congressional oversight.

Powell's staff put Hollings' letter online, as they are required to do by federal sunshine laws. The memo arrived as a Microsoft Word file -- which EFF then downloaded and analyzed. Word stashes the identity of a document's author in the file metadata, which is how EFF discovered that the document had been written by a staffer at the MPAA.

This was truly remarkable. Hollings was a powerful committee chairman, one who had taken immense sums of money from the industries he was supposed to be regulating. It's easy to be cynical about this kind of thing, but it's genuinely unforgivable: Politicians draw a public salary to sit in public office and work for the public good. They're supposed to be working for us, not their donors.

But we all know that this isn't true. Politicians are happy to give special favors to their pals in industry. However, the Hollings memo was beyond the pale. Staffers for the MPAA were writing Hollings' memos, memos that Hollings then signed and mailed off to the heads of major governmental agencies.

The best part was that the legal eagles at the MPAA were wrong. The FCC took "Hollings'" advice and enacted a Broadcast Flag regulation that was almost identical to the proposal from the BPDG, turning themselves into America's "device czars," able to burden any digital technology with "robustness," "compliance," and "revocation rules." The rule lasted just long enough for the DC Circuit Court of Appeals to strike it down and slap the FCC for grabbing unprecedented jurisdiction over the devices in our living rooms.

So ended the saga of the Broadcast Flag. More or less. In the years since the Flag was proposed, there have been several attempts to reintroduce it through legislation, all failed. And as more and more innovative, open devices like the Neuros OSD enter the market, it gets harder and harder to imagine that Americans will accept a mandate that takes away all that functionality.

But the spirit of the Broadcast Flag lives on. DRM consortia are all the rage now -- outfits like AACS LA, the folks who control the DRM in Blu-Ray and HD-DVD, are thriving and making headlines by issuing fatwas against people who publish their secret integers. In Europe, a DRM consortium working under the auspices of the Digital Video Broadcasters Forum (DVB) has just shipped a proposed standard for digital TV DRM that makes the Broadcast Flag look like the work of patchouli-scented infohippies. The DVB proposal would give DRM consortium the ability to define what is and isn't a valid "household" for the purposes of sharing your video within your "household's devices." It limits how long you're allowed to pause a video for, and allows for restrictions to be put in place for hundreds of years, longer than any copyright system in the world would protect any work for.

If all this stuff seems a little sneaky, underhanded, and even illegal to you, you're not alone. When representatives of nearly all the world's entertainment, technology, broadcast, satellite, and cable companies gather in a room to collude to cripple their offerings, limit their innovation, and restrict the market, regulators take notice.

That's why the EU is taking a hard look at HD-DVD and Blu-Ray. These systems aren't designed: They're governed, and the governors are shadowy group of offshore giants who answer to no one -- not even their own members! I once called the DVD-Copy Control Association (DVD-CCA) on behalf of a Time-Warner magazine, *Popular Science*, for a comment about their DRM. Not only wouldn't they allow me to speak to a spokesman, the person who denied my request also refused to be identified.

The sausage factory grinds away, but today, more activists than ever are finding ways to participate in the negotiations, slowing them up, making them account for themselves to the public. And so long as you, the technology-buying public, pay attention to what's going on, the activists will continue to hold back the tide.

$$$$

[Originally published as "A Behind-The-Scenes Look At How DRM Becomes Law," *InformationWeek*, July 11, 2007.]

PIRATES
LAWRENCE LESSIG

If "piracy" means using the creative property of others without their permission— if "if value, then right" is true— then the history of the content industry is a history of piracy. Every important sector of "big media" today— film, records, radio, and cable TV— was born of a kind of piracy so defined. The consistent story is how last generation's pirates join this generation's country club— until now.

Film

The film industry of Hollywood was built by fleeing pirates.[1] Creators and directors migrated from the East Coast to California in the early twentieth century in part to escape controls that patents granted the inventor of film making, Thomas Edison. These controls were exercised through a monopoly "trust," the Motion Pictures Patents Company, and were based on Thomas Edison's creative property— patents. Edison formed the MPPC to exercise the rights this creative property gave him, and the MPPC was serious about the control it demanded.

As one commentator tells one part of the story,

No Safe Harbor

A January 1909 deadline was set for all companies to comply with the license. By February, unlicensed outlaws, who referred to themselves as independents protested the trust and carried on business without submitting to the Edison monopoly. In the summer of 1909 the independent movement was in full-swing, with producers and theater owners using illegal equipment and imported film stock to create their own underground market.

With the country experiencing a tremendous expansion in the number of nickelodeons, the Patents Company reacted to the independent movement by forming a strong-arm subsidiary known as the General Film Company to block the entry of non-licensed independents. With coercive tactics that have become legendary, General Film confiscated unlicensed equipment, discontinued product supply to theaters which showed unlicensed films, and effectively monopolized distribution with the acquisition of all U.S. film exchanges, except for the one owned by the independent William Fox who defied the Trust even after his license was revoked. [2]

The Napsters of those days, the "independents," were companies like Fox. And no less than today, these independents were vigorously resisted.

"Shooting was disrupted by machinery stolen, and 'accidents' resulting in loss of negatives, equipment, buildings and sometimes life and limb frequently occurred."[3] That led the independents to flee the East Coast. California was remote enough from Edison's reach that filmmakers there could pirate his inventions without fear of the law. And the leaders of Hollywood film making, Fox most prominently, did just that.

Of course, California grew quickly, and the effective enforcement of federal law eventually spread west. But because patents grant the patent holder a truly "limited" monopoly (just seventeen years at that time), by the time enough federal marshals appeared, the patents had expired. A new industry had been born, in part from the piracy of Edison's creative property.

Recorded Music

The record industry was born of another kind of piracy, though to see how requires a bit of detail about the way the law regulates music. At the time that Edison and Henri Fourneaux invented machines for reproducing music (Edison the phonograph, Fourneaux the player piano), the law gave composers the exclusive right to control copies of their music and the exclusive right to control public performances of their music. In other words, in 1900, if I wanted a copy of Phil Russel's 1899 hit "Happy Mose," the law said I would have to pay for the right to get a copy of the musical score, and I would also have to pay for the right to perform it publicly.

But what if I wanted to record "Happy Mose," using Edison's phonograph or Fourneaux's player piano? Here the law stumbled. It was clear enough that I would have to buy any copy of the musical score that I performed in making this recording. And it was clear enough that I would have to pay for any public performance of the work I was recording.

But it wasn't totally clear that I would have to pay for a "public performance" if I recorded the song in my own house (even today, you don't owe the Beatles anything if you sing their songs in the shower), or if I recorded the song from memory (copies in your brain are not— yet— regulated by copyright law). So if I simply sang the song into a recording device in the privacy of my own home, it wasn't clear that I owed the composer anything. And more importantly, it wasn't clear whether I owed the composer anything if I then made copies of those recordings.

Because of this gap in the law, then, I could effectively pirate someone else's song without paying its composer anything.

The composers (and publishers) were none too happy about this capacity to pirate. As South Dakota senator Alfred Kittredge put it,

No Safe Harbor

Imagine the injustice of the thing. A composer writes a song or an opera. A publisher buys at great expense the rights to the same and copyrights it. Along come the phonographic companies and companies who cut music rolls and deliberately steal the work of the brain of the composer and publisher without any regard for [their] rights.[4]

The innovators who developed the technology to record other people's works were "sponging upon the toil, the work, the talent, and genius of American composers,"[5] and the "music publishing industry" was thereby "at the complete mercy of this one pirate." [6] As John Philip Sousa put it, in as direct a way as possible, "When they make money out of my pieces, I want a share of it."[7]

These arguments have familiar echoes in the wars of our day. So, too, do the arguments on the other side. The innovators who developed the player piano argued that "it is perfectly demonstrable that the introduction of automatic music players has not deprived any composer of anything he had before their introduction." Rather, the machines increased the sales of sheet music.[8] In any case, the innovators argued, the job of Congress was "to consider first the interest of [the public], whom they represent, and whose servants they are." "All talk about 'theft,'" the general counsel of the American Graphophone Company wrote, "is the merest claptrap, for there exists no property in ideas musical, literary or artistic, except as defined by statute."[9]

The law soon resolved this battle in favor of the composer *and* the recording artist. Congress amended the law to make sure that composers would be paid for the "mechanical reproductions" of their music. But rather than simply granting the composer complete control over the right to make mechanical reproductions, Congress gave recording artists a right to record the music, at a price set by Congress, once the composer allowed it to be recorded once. This is the part of copyright law that makes cover songs possible. Once a composer authorizes a recording of his song, others are free to record the same song, so long as they pay the original composer a fee set by the law.

American law ordinarily calls this a "compulsory license," but I will refer to it as a "statutory license." A statutory license is a license whose key terms are set by law. After Congress's amendment of the Copyright Act in 1909, record companies were free to distribute copies of recordings so long as they paid the composer (or copyright holder) the fee set by the statute.

This is an exception within the law of copyright. When John Grisham writes a novel, a publisher is free to publish that novel only if Grisham gives the publisher permission. Grisham, in turn, is free to charge whatever he wants for that permission. The price to publish Grisham is thus set by Grisham, and copyright law ordinarily says you have no permission to use Grisham's work except with permission of Grisham.

But the law governing recordings gives recording artists less. And thus, in effect, the law *subsidizes* the recording industry through a kind of piracy— by giving recording artists a weaker right than it otherwise gives creative authors. The Beatles have less control over their creative work than Grisham does. And the beneficiaries of this less control are the recording industry and the public. The recording industry gets something of value for less than it otherwise would pay; the public gets access to a much wider range of musical creativity. Indeed, Congress was quite explicit about its reasons for granting this right. Its fear was the monopoly power of rights holders, and that that power would stifle follow-on creativity.[10]

While the recording industry has been quite coy about this recently, historically it has been quite a supporter of the statutory license for records. As a 1967 report from the House Committee on the Judiciary relates, *the record producers argued vigorously that the compulsory license system must be retained. They asserted that the record industry is a half-billion-dollar business of great economic importance in the United States and throughout the world; records today are the principal means of disseminating music, and this creates special problems, since performers need unhampered access to musical material on nondiscriminatory terms. Historically, the record producers pointed out, there were no recording rights before 1909 and the 1909 statute adopted the compulsory license as a deliberate anti-monopoly condition on the grant of these rights. They argue that the result has been an outpouring of recorded music, with the public being given lower prices, improved quality, and a greater choice.[11]*

By limiting the rights musicians have, by partially pirating their creative work, the record producers, and the public, benefit.

Radio

Radio was also born of piracy.

When a radio station plays a record on the air, that constitutes a "public performance" of the composer's work.[12] As I described above, the law gives the composer (or copyright holder) an exclusive right to public performances of his work. The radio station thus owes the composer money for that performance.

But when the radio station plays a record, it is not only performing a copy of the *composer's* work. The radio station is also performing a copy of the *recording artist's* work. It's one thing to have "Happy Birthday" sung on the radio by the local children's choir; it's quite another to have it sung by the Rolling Stones or Lyle Lovett. The recording artist is adding to the value of the composition performed on the radio station.

And if the law were perfectly consistent, the radio station would have to pay the recording artist for his work, just as it pays the composer of the music for his work.

But it doesn't. Under the law governing radio performances, the radio station does not have to pay the recording artist. The radio station need only pay the composer. The radio station thus gets a bit of something for nothing. It gets to perform the recording artist's work for free, even if it must pay the composer something for the privilege of playing the song.

This difference can be huge. Imagine you compose a piece of music. Imagine it is your first. You own the exclusive right to authorize public performances of that music. So if Madonna wants to sing your song in public, she has to get your permission.

Imagine she does sing your song, and imagine she likes it a lot. She then decides to make a recording of your song, and it becomes a top hit. Under our law, every time a radio station plays your song, you get some money. But Madonna gets nothing, save the indirect effect on the sale of her CDs. The public performance of her recording is not a "protected" right. The radio station thus gets to *pirate* the value of Madonna's work without paying her anything.

No doubt, one might argue that, on balance, the recording artists benefit. On average, the promotion they get is worth more than the performance rights they give up. Maybe. But even if so, the law ordinarily gives the creator the right to make this choice. By making the choice for him or her, the law gives the radio station the right to take something for nothing.

Cable TV

Cable TV was also born of a kind of piracy.

When cable entrepreneurs first started wiring communities with cable television in 1948, most refused to pay broadcasters for the content that they echoed to their customers. Even when the cable companies started selling access to television broadcasts, they refused to pay for what they sold. Cable companies were thus Napsterizing broad-

casters' content, but more egregiously than anything Napster ever did
— Napster never charged for the content it enabled others to give
away.

Broadcasters and copyright owners were quick to attack this theft.
Rosel Hyde, chairman of the FCC, viewed the practice as a kind of
"unfair and potentially destructive competition."[13] There may have
been a "public interest" in spreading the reach of cable TV, but as
Douglas Anello, general counsel to the National Association of
Broadcasters, asked Senator Quentin Burdick during testimony, "Does
public interest dictate that you use somebody else's property?"[14] As
another broadcaster put it,

*The extraordinary thing about the CATV business is that it is the only business I
know of where the product that is being sold is not paid for.[15]*

Again, the demand of the copyright holders seemed reasonable
enough:

*All we are asking for is a very simple thing, that people who now take our property
for nothing pay for it. We are trying to stop piracy and I don't think there is any
lesser word to describe it. I think there are harsher words which would fit it.[16]*

These were "free-ride[rs]," Screen Actor's Guild president Charlton
Heston said, who were "depriving actors of compensation."[17] But
again, there was another side to the debate. As Assistant Attorney
General Edwin Zimmerman put it,

*Our point here is that unlike the problem of whether you have any copyright
protection at all, the problem here is whether copyright holders who are already
compensated, who already have a monopoly, should be permitted to extend that
monopoly. . . . The question here is how much compensation they should have and
how far back they should carry their right to compensation.[18]*

Copyright owners took the cable companies to court. Twice the
Supreme Court held that the cable companies owed the copyright

owners nothing.

It took Congress almost thirty years before it resolved the question of whether cable companies had to pay for the content they "pirated." In the end, Congress resolved this question in the same way that it resolved the question about record players and player pianos. Yes, cable companies would have to pay for the content that they broadcast; but the price they would have to pay was not set by the copyright owner.

The price was set by law, so that the broadcasters couldn't exercise veto power over the emerging technologies of cable. Cable companies thus built their empire in part upon a "piracy" of the value created by broadcasters' content.

These separate stories sing a common theme. If "piracy" means using value from someone else's creative property without permission from that creator—as it is increasingly described today[19]— then *every* industry affected by copyright today is the product and beneficiary of a certain kind of piracy. Film, records, radio, cable TV. . . . The list is long and could well be expanded. Every generation welcomes the pirates from the last. Every generation—until now.

[This essay was originally published in the author's book *Free Culture.*]

QUESTIONS CONCERNING COPYRIGHT
BRAD HALL

In my years with the United States Pirate Party, I have been interviewed by various news outlets and students doing papers on third parties for various classes. I always answer student questions whenever such an e-mail appears in my inbox. Below are a sampling of their questions and my responses to them. I hope these students all received A's for their effort. Also, I am a big anime/manga fan, and that definitely comes out in this series of questions and answers. While this essay was originally written in 2010 and has existed for some time on the main USPP website and elsewhere, this version is newly updated.

1. Do you personally acquire digital media through file sharing?: Downloading copyrighted material breaks several laws, and it is not the Pirate Party's goal to break the law, simply to bring the law's perspective into the digital information age.

2. How would content producers profit, if their media is being provided free of charge?: The easiest way would be advertising. The people who make the songs that are the most listened to and the most downloaded or whatever, would receive the larger share of the revenue pie. Of course, as a friend pointed out to me previously, "Okay, advertising. Where does that money come from? As they say, every action has an equal and opposite reaction. You're funded with advertising, someone else lost that advertising dollar."

While an advertising-supported model has its limits, there are several models that have worked well for several companies/people.

Anime Network and Crunchyroll both have a system in place where you can watch some anime for free. Then you can watch more and other anime for a price. The price ranges from $7 per month to a yearly pass of $70 per year. I have no idea how many subscribers they get at any price. They also host a few advertisements. I have no idea how many or how much money those generate. Presumably it's enough to keep them in business.

Kodansha recently came up with an idea of releasing manga (Japanese comic books) as a series of iPod/iPhone apps. It's a great idea, but there is that one major hurdle to cross: Apple itself. Apple is the gatekeeper for everything that is sold on the iTunes Store. If Apple does not approve of something, it does not get sold.

Selling on Amazon's Kindle ebook store would be another possibility. The overhead is lower for an Internet-based store than it is for a brick-and-mortar store. Also, there would be no physical objects to ship, so manga created for distribution on a Kindle (or other ebook reader) could retail for a lower price.

There is a comic called *Megatokyo* (www.megatokyo.com). It's an American comic done in a "manga style." Usually every Monday, Wednesday, and Friday, one page is uploaded to the site. The comic has a pile of followers, including myself. The way the author monetizes it is by selling a "low bandwidth version" (book) and shirts and other things that pop up in the comic.

Every page that has ever been uploaded to the *Megatokyo* site is still there so anyone can go back and read the series from the beginning at any time. This is particularly helpful for new fans who want to join the story.

Though, the only way that would work with manga is if the original writers release it online the same way. Of course these pages would have to be translated into nearly every language that the fans speak to ensure they keep coming back to the primary site and not some third party site that offers the pages translated to their language.

The difference between *Megatokyo* and any other manga is *Megatokyo* was made from the beginning to be a webcomic. If you read today's page and get frustrated and want to read the next page, or the next chapter, tough. You have to wait for the page along with everyone else. You can't go to some website and download the entirety of the series.

While flipping through an issue of one of my favorite manga series, *Loveless*, I can find no t-shirts that Soubi or Ritsuka wear that make me say "Oooh! I want that shirt!" though, some weirdo fangirls might go for the cat ears or something. Maybe a messenger bag. Every series has a messenger bag. Or maybe make a tie-in MMO.

In *Loveless*, the villains meet up in *Wisdom Resurrection*, a fictional MMORPG that appears to be based on *Final Fantasy XI*. That's where they hold some of their meetings. Maybe they could make an MMO based on that. Maybe take a cue from Turbine and make it free-to-play, but make money via micro-transactions.

Turbine is a company that makes video games. Two of their game series, D*ungeons & Dragons Online* and *Lord of the Rings Online* used to be MMORPGs (Massively Multiplayer Online Role Playing Games) that operated under a subscription model, for so much money per month, you could play. Starting in 2009 Turbine started making these games free-to-play. You could still pay a monthly fee to receive certain advantages such as the ability to carry more gold and items, but you could play the games, to their completion, without paying a cent if you wanted. Many new players flocked to the games.

The third idea is to create a Hulu-like site where everything is free and available from all the major manufacturers. Force people to watch an ad or read an ad or whatever for x number of pages viewed.

The other problem with manga is this: "What's good?" If you walk into a Books-A-Million any day of the week, you will find a pile of manga titles. Manga isn't like a "funny book" where you can pick up any issue and know what's going on. There's a story. If I picked up *Loveless* volume six and read it without having read the previous five volumes, I'd have no idea what was going on.

"Thanks grandma… *Full Metal Alchemist* volume 73… thanks… yes grandma, this is one of them Japanese manga comics." Never mind the fact I hadn't read volume 1-72.

With a manga, you have to read about 2 or 3 volumes to figure out what the story is. That's a cost of around $30 and who knows how many weeks/months/years of waiting for new volume to come out. And even then? Who knows. With 8 volumes of *Loveless*, I have spent $80, if each volume costs $10.

For $80, I could buy every Stephen King book I've not read yet.

As of this writing, *Naruto*, the most popular manga series currently in circulation is up to volume 58. Each volume retails for $10, then the entire run would cost $580, and that's before taxes. What kind of person has that kind of disposable income?

I was happy when *Shonen Jump* was released in the US several years ago. *Shonen Jump* is a manga anthology, each issue contains several chapters of a few different manga in it. I bought a subscription and had it active for a few years. I started to care less and less about it once *Sandland* concluded. Then I let it lapse. I have no idea what's in it now.

Like I said, they don't make it easy for people to find a new manga to get into. Why spend money on a series you might hate when you can pop onto a website and read a few chapters of it, heck, why not read the whole thing?

A coalition of comic book and manga publishers in the US and Japan has been pushing for litigation against at least 30 illegal scanlation websites.[1]

Scanlation is a portmandeau of "scan" and "translation" it refers to the act of obtaining the original (usually Japanese) language release of a manga (either by physically obtaining a copy or downloading a raw copy, a copy that is still in its original language).

Diehard fans translate their favorite series and release it on one of several popular scanlation websites. Manga isn't the only thing that can be scanlated, though, when it comes to anime, the word used is fansub.

Sure, one of the manga scanlation sites that's under attack by the coalition is a Google Top 1000 website with page views that hover in the billions, but the questions are:

A. How much manga on that site is available commercially in the US? I talked to a friend of mine and found that he enjoyed a certain manga. Only nine volumes of that series were legitimately translated and released in the US, out of 20 volumes altogether. Then, for whatever reason, the US company that was legitimately translating and releasing it, canceled it. There are still 11 volumes unreleased in English. The friend went on to tell me how he read the rest of the series online as it was the only place that he could read the entire series. Oh, and that series had to be translated into English by a fan who enjoyed that series as well. I felt my friend's pain, as the company that had been releasing *Loveless* in the US decided to drop their license.

That's just an example of something we used to have, but don't have any more. What about the series that never came out here at all?

B. Would the people who read the manga online have bought it? This goes for the ones not released here as well as the ones that are. It's the old question about downloading MP3s. Is it really "theft" if no physical item was removed?

Clearly there is a massive demand for easily obtainable manga and anime.

There are several authors who make pretty good money by releasing their material for free on their websites while also selling books. Cory Doctorow, an author (who also has an essay in this collection) does just that. By having the digital version of a book advertise for the printed version, it allows his work to spread further than it would have otherwise.

With today's print-on-demand companies, no one has to deal with a big publisher. This book you're reading right now, *No Safe Harbor*, was published as a free-to-download PDF. But, a print-on-demand version was also created. These POD companies print books as they are sold, so there is no warehouse to maintain a backlog of unsold books.

If we take that idea back to manga, it would be incredibly easy for a US or Japanese manga publisher to release content on a website for reading, and then have a system set up with a print-on-demand publisher to print only the copies of the full volume that are ordered by either bookstores or people. Of course, the thing that most likely stands in the way for such a system is rights and licensing of materials across several countries, hiring of translators, and other support people, as well as fear.

Fear?

Yes, fear. Most companies know how to make money doing what they are doing. They are afraid to try something new for fear that their house of cards could tumble down. They fear that which is new. Song writers feared player pianos, musicians feared radio, television broadcasters feared the VCR, music publishers feared Napster. It's a cycle of fear.

3. Why do you think piracy is illegal?: The idea that sharing anything online is piracy is absurd. Actual piracy requires forceful and aggressive acts, committed against those who would keep a cargo safe from harm. The cargo in this case is the freedom to act. We would take it from those who jealously guard it for themselves and divide it amongst everyone in the country.

The Pirate Party wants to "raid" the law and "carry away" (repeal) laws which do not serve those on our metaphorical boat. The trick of it is: we're all in the same boat. It is in service to those on our boat (the United States) that we aim to help.

We are not willing to accept that file sharing should be banned (and will take steps– once we have party members in office– to ensure that any laws in this regard are adamantly opposed, since technology isn't the problem, but rather education about what its proper use is). On the other hand, we do agree that there is a significant amount of wrong being done to our rights in the name of protecting those whose sole aim for over 50 years has been the control and manipulation of human minds. Brainwashing our population is against our national interest in maintaining a democracy.

4. Should file sharers be punished? Should file sharers who sell the content for a profit be punished?: Back in the day, before the Internet. People would create "mix tapes" these were audio tapes that someone had painstakingly recorded a few songs from several vinyl records or other tapes to. Typically these were given to friends, not "friend" in the Internet sense, but friend in the local sense. You could really only physically hand these mix tapes to people you knew in person. These tapes were generally given as a kind of sampler, like a "this is the kind of music I'm in to, and I think you might dig it as well" kind of thing.

These tapes were given freely to people, and usually didn't contain more than one or two songs by a particular artist. To the purveyors of mix tapes, these were not only seen as somewhat free advertising for artists, they were believed to be fair use (which is a tricky thing to actually prove), and then there's the Audio Home Recording Act, which made the companies that created and sold blank audio tapes and tape deck recorders pay royalties to music writers and music publishers, whether or not the tapes were used to copy music. So right there, that was almost like the government saying it was legal to make mix tapes. (However, that does not make the old Napster or burning CDs on your computer legal).[2]

But, the second part of the question has to do with the selling of such content for profit. That is undeniably wrong. In November, 2010, I wrote a USPP newsletter item about a trip I made to the flea market. On this particular trip, I found a man selling obviously bootlegged DVDs on recordable media with the names of the films written on them with a Sharpie. That guy was breaking the law.[3]

He should be punished, as should other people who try to sell other people's content for money. He is just as guilty as someone who would rent out the use of your car without you knowing, and without you receiving any of the proceeds thereof.

Okay, that's probably a bad analogy, but it's still not good.

As a counterpoint, I will say this: I have read that the only group who can use file sharing without problem is radio broadcasters as they do have to catalog each song and artist they play and pay royalties to the appropriate music writers and publishers organizations, so even if they download a song to play on the air, they're still paying the original writer and publisher of the music.

A side note, notice I said nothing about the person who actually sings the song. Back when the royalty rates were first organized for these things, it was decreed that the song writer receive a portion and the song publisher receive a portion as the song itself was seen as an advertisement for the singer (and their band)'s albums. Of course, there are some songs that were written by the singer, so in that case the singer does get a royalty.

5. Do you think we can come up with a compromise to current file sharing laws?: Before you can come up with a compromise to current file sharing laws, you first have to figure out the why. Why do people share files? There are a pile of reasons. One is money, we're in a financial crisis. People are losing jobs left and right, the amount of disposable income people have is decreasing, yet the price of content is increasing rapidly.

A number of people believe that content should be free and easily accessible. One way for that to happen is through an advertising supported model. Several years ago, one such service, called Ruckus existed for several years. It was only open to people who could sign up with a .edu email address, ostensibly, college students. You could download songs, for free. New songs, and even older songs, were added all the time. It was great! I loved it.

There was a few problems though: while you could download songs to your computer and play them offline, you could not remove them from your computer or burn to a CD or transfer to your iPod or other music playing device. They were locked to your computer, and so were you if you wanted to play your music.

The song files also only had a life of 30 days, you had to log back into the Ruckus website and Ruckus Media Player in order to renew the license on the songs.

That was a problem I could live with. But, then one day in 2009, the party ended. Officially, Ruckus said the problem was "overcrowding" –

clearly the demand was there for a free music service. Too much demand.

There are two more free music services that recently came online, Spotify and Pandora. I have not had enough time using those services to pass judgment on them.

6. Do you think the laws should adapt to evolving technology?:
Yes. The problem with the current laws of the United States is that the vast majority of them were written in the 1700s or had lobbyists and corporate interests in mind, and not the average citizen. The original term of copyright was 14 years, renewable to a further 14 years for a maximum of 28 years. Copyright now is "70 years after the death of author. If a work of corporate authorship, 95 years from publication or 120 years from creation, whichever expires first" that's not exactly a "limited time" while technically, it is, but for the vast majority of the people alive today, we will all be dead in 120 years, so to us, that's not a limited time, that's a lifetime, plus several years. I would love for copyright to return to its original 14-year term.[4]

7. If you were an artist, would you support free distribution of your content?: Yes. I intend to release most, if not all material I have created under a Creative Commons license, like the one this book uses. However, several years ago, Prince released his latest album, not in stores, but in the newspaper. Anyone who bought a copy of "The Mail on Sunday" received a free copy of his latest album, *Planet Earth*. Also, he had concert dates for 21 days in London that completely sold out, most likely due to his free CD advertising.

While this is a different kind of "sharing" than the kind the Internet is blamed for, the principle is the same: Would any of the people who received the free album bought it before? Would they have gone to Prince's show too?

8. Do you believe piracy is stealing?: I believe I mentioned it previously, but, everyone who pirates an album, would they have bought that album had the pirated version not been available to them? I think not, at least not in every sense.

Downloading an album is different than walking into Best Buy or where ever, grabbing a CD, and walking out of a store without paying for it.

When you download an album, you're just making a digital copy of it. Nothing has been removed. The original copy of that digital file is still on whatever computer it originally came from.

But when you go into a store and walk out without paying for the CD hidden in your jacket pocket, that is stealing. The retail industry has a word for it, "shrink" as in "shrinking profits" – it might take a while before the store realizes the CD has been stolen. As long as their computers say they still have one copy of an album on the shelves, they will not order more as they believe they still have one in stock. In this way, stealing one album could in turn lead to further lost sales than just one CD.

9. Who benefits the most from piracy?: There are two sides to this coin. On one side, let's say you like Band X, you download all of their albums, you give your friends copies of those copies, and those copies propagate exponentially. On one hand, Band X now has a pile of fans, every band wants a pile of fans, right? But, on the other hand, now that you and a pile of friends you've never met have copies of Band X's albums (for free, mind you), Band X is showing that they haven't sold many albums because you and your "friends" have downloaded them. Why would Band X make more music when they don't make any money from it? What record label would allow a band that doesn't make money to release more albums? In the end, the record label decides not to renew their contract.

However, on the other side of the coin, the band now has many fans. These fans could channel their love of the band into ticket sales for a live tour. Several years ago the British band Radiohead left their record label, EMI, and proceeded to record a new album. Instead of releasing it as a CD, the band decided instead to release it on the internet using a "pay what you want" pricing structure. You could pay nothing for it, or you could pay a penny, or you could pay considerably more. The band went on record as saying they had made more money on the sales of that album than they had receieved for the digital sales of all their previous albums combined.

That marked the start of the self-releasing superstar band. Recently Hawthorne Heights and others have left their labels to become independent bands. While this does not stop piracy of their albums, without a record label, the band keeps more money of the sales they do make and are freer to make the artisitic decisions they want, not what upper management wants.

10. Do you agree with Google's censorship of terms related to filesharing (torrent, utorrent, bittorrent, rapidshare, megaupload) in the autofill and instant features?: What Google is trying to do is move the blame away from themselves in this matter. By having "torrent" pop up in an auto complete window would almost be like Google suggesting someone to download something using bittorrent. But, Google's results themselves have no qualms about filling the results pages full of Rapidshare and Megaupload links. So basically, Google is trying to cover its rear in that it wouldn't "suggest" those words to you, but won't stop you from clicking on links from those sites. If it did stop users, then that would raise several net neutrality issues that Google does not want to contend with, such as controlling where users go online.

11. Do you agree with the claims that piracy is hurting the music industry?: I believe I touched on this item before in the last question. But yes, I would say piracy is having an effect on the music industry.

How big of an impact? I don't know. And I'm willing to doubt the information and research the music industry is pushing forward on the matter. How can they know how many copies of a given album would sell if the Internet didn't exist?

There's many reasons (and possibilities) why the music industry is hurting. One could be lack of good music, of course, everyone has a different idea of what good music is. And that's one thing that could also be hurting the music industry: The glut of musicians. Back in "the day" there were fewer genres of music and the channels to get to that music was narrow as well. Everyone was listening to the same bands, so everyone bought the same records. You had Rock, Country (far different than the Country of today), Folk (which could be considered an offshoot of Country), R&B, Classical, and maybe a few others I can't think of off the top of my head.

Today, just by looking at what I have on my shelf (I am an avid music lover and have over 200 CDs and I've not counted how much I have on vinyl) we have: Classic Rock, Contemporary Rock, Metal, Emo, Alternative, Trance, Video Game music, Eurobeat, J-Pop, Para Para, Canadian Folk, Finnish Prog Rock, American Prog Rock, Canadian Prog Rock, The Beatles (so good they have their own genre), Punk, Hardcore, Vocaloid, Surfer, Rap, R&B, Gangsta Rap, Screamo, Film soundtracks, Broadway play soundtracks, etc, and even some of those genres have subgenres that splinter infinitely.

So you see, a kind of splintering has occurred in music, we have more of it and getting more every day (or every Tuesday if you're going by store release dates). I would love to see a study that seeks to see if this "hurting of the music industry" could be explained by this splintering. Bands aren't selling millions of copies of albums anymore, but a few hundred thousand, if they're lucky.

12. How do you view the current court cases of Joel Tenenbaum vs the RIAA and Jammie Thomas vs the RIAA?: Thomas was the first person to be brought to trial for downloading music. She was brought to trial over 24 songs. The case kept being repealed and the amount of money figured for the settlement kept changing. At one trial she was told to pay $222,000. At another trial, $54,000. At a third trial, she was told to pay $1.5 million. At the $1.5 million dollar level, that amounts to $62,500 per song.

Per song?

Twenty-four songs, right? Okay, that's around 2 CDs worth of music, give or take. What if she shoplifted this music instead? What if she shoplifted however many CDs she'd need to steal to come up with the 24 songs she was brought to trial over?

In Florida, if caught for shoplifting an item that costs less than $300 the maximum fine would be a fine of up to $500 and/or two months in jail for the first offense. Even the penalty for a 3rd offense isn't as severe as having to pay over a million dollars. In that case, the crime is upgraded to a felony, a fine of up to $5000 and/or five years in prison. [5]

That's outrageous.

Not outrageous in the sense that Florida's fine and prison sentence is insane, it isn't. It's that the law in this country right now seems to think that if a computer was used in any way to commit a crime it makes it far more serious than if a computer was not used.

These were some great questions. Given that I've put these on the website (and this book) where anyone can read them now, I'd love to see some new questions from students.

Clearly there are far more ideas for this kind of thing than I have put forth. This is just a start.

THIS GENE IS YOUR GENE
KEMBREW MCLEOD

"This gene is your gene," sang Francis Collins, playfully reworking an old Woody Guthrie song, with electric guitar in hand. "This gene is my gene," he continued, backed up by the lumbering roar of a middle-aged rock band. This was no ordinary club gig; he was singing at a post–press conference party for scientists. Collins was the man who headed up the Human Genome Project (HGP), funded by the National Institutes of Health, and he was trying to make an ethical and political point. Since the mid-1990s, Collins' HGP had raced against a private effort to map the human genome in order to make our genetic information freely accessible, not privately owned and patented by a handful of corporations. Any scientist could examine HGP's genome map for free— unlike the Celera Genomics' privately owned draft, which was published with strings attached.[1] Over the din, Collins chided his competitors in song by genetically modifying Guthrie's lyrics:

This draft is your draft, this draft is my draft,

And it's a free draft, no charge to see draft.

It's our instruction book, so come on, have a look,

United States Pirate Party
This draft was made for you and me

Dr. Francis Collins reworked "This Land Is Your Land" to argue that genetic information should be freely available to the scientific community. However, his use of that Woody Guthrie song was sadly ironic, on multiple levels. "This Land Is Your Land" is a song written by an unabashed socialist as a paean to communal property: "This land was made for you *and* me." Another key lyric goes, "A sign was painted 'Private Property' but on the backside it didn't say nothin'." The folk-song tradition from which Guthrie emerged valued the open borrowing of lyrics and melodies; culture was meant to be freely created and re-created in a democratic, participatory way.

If this was so, then why was Collins' use of "This Land Is Your Land" painfully ironic? Even though it was written over sixty years ago, the song is, to quote Woody Guthrie himself, still "private property." Guthrie based the melody of "This Land Is Your Land" on the Carter Family's 1928 recording "Little Darlin' Pal of Mine," which in turn was derived from a nineteenth-century gospel song, "Oh, My Loving Brother."[2] This means that, in the twenty-first century, the publishing company that owns the late Guthrie's music can earn money from a song about communal property, which was itself based on a tune that is over a century old. Far more disturbing, Guthrie's publishing company prevents musicians from releasing altered, updated lyrical versions of that song. We won't be hearing Collins' mutated "This Gene Is Your Gene" anytime soon.

What's the connection, you might be wondering, between folk music and genetic research? Although obviously very different endeavors, the practitioners of both used to value the open sharing of information (i.e., melodies or scientific data). In these communities, "texts" were often considered common property, but today this *concept has been fundamentally altered by the process of privatization,* that is, the belief that shared public resources— sometimes referred to by economists and social scientists as the commons— can be better managed by private industries. And in recent years, there's been a significant erosion of both the *cultural* commons and the *genetic* commons, resulting in a shrinking of the public domain. The fact that folk melodies and lyrics are now privately owned rather than shared resources is a depressing example of how our cultural commons is being fenced off. As for the genetic commons, the patenting of human and plant genes is but the furthest logical extension of privatization— taken at times to illogical lengths.

MAKING FOLK MUSIC

One year, I was taking a shuttle van back from the airport, glad to be back in Iowa City but exhausted from the Christmas holidays and feeling mute. However, I was alone with a driver who obviously wanted to chat, so I answered his questions about what I do. I mentioned my interest in music, which got the full attention of Jim Bazzell— the grizzled, fifty-something man behind the wheel. It turned out that Bazzell's father had been in a band called Jimmy and the Westerners, one of the many country-music combos that roamed the land in the 1940s and 1950s. They once performed at Nashville's Grand Ole Opry and had their own radio show, though the group mainly made a living playing in honky-tonk bars around the Southwest."My dad couldn't read music and would play by ear," says Bazzell. "I remember my mom would scramble to write down song lyrics as they came on the radio." He chuckles, "Of course, she'd get a lot of 'em wrong because she couldn't write as fast as they sang, so my dad would just make up the lyrics he didn't know."

This kind of improvisation used to be a common practice, especially in folk and country circles where lyrics and melodies were treated as raw materials that could be reshaped and molded in the moment. When writing my last book, for instance, I happened to be listening to a lot of old country music, and I noticed that *six* country songs shared the same vocal melody, including Hank Thompson's "Wild Side of Life."[2] In his exhaustively researched book, *Country: The Twisted Roots of Rock 'n' Roll,* Nick Toches documented that the melody these songs used was both "ancient and British." It's unlikely that the writers of these songs simply ran out of melodic ideas and decided to pillage someone else's music. It wasn't artistic laziness. Rather, it's probable that these six country songwriters, the majority of whom grew up during the first half of the twentieth century, felt comfortable borrowing folk melodies. They probably didn't think twice about it.

This was also a time when more people knew how to play musical instruments, like Bazzell's family, which performed small gigs at local hospitals and the like. His dad was proficient on fiddle and guitar —"any stringed instrument, really," Jim says— and the kids learned to play at an early age, as did his mom. The stories he told reminded me of the song "Daddy Sang Bass," which Carl Perkins wrote and Johnny Cash popularized. "Mama sang tenor," the song's chorus continued."Me and little brother would join right in there."It describes how the singer's parents are now in heaven and how one day he'll rejoin the family circle in song, concluding, "No, the circle won't be broken . . ."

The chorus makes an overt reference to an important folk song that dates back to the nineteenth century: "Will the Circle Be Unbroken," which the Carter Family made famous. Starting in the 1930s, Woody Guthrie drew direct inspiration from a lot of songs associated with the Carter Family, recycling their melodies to write his own pro-union songs. For example, Guthrie wrote in his journal of song ideas: "Tune of 'Will the Circle Be Unbroken'—will the union stay unbroken. Needed: a sassy tune for a scab song."

Guthrie also discovered that a Baptist hymn performed by the Carter Family, "This World Is Not My Home," was popular in migrant farm worker camps, but he felt the lyrics were counterproductive politically. The song didn't deal with the day-to-day miseries forced upon the workers by the rich and instead told them they'd be rewarded for their patience in the next life:

No Safe Harbor

This world is not my home

I'm just a-passing through

My treasures are laid up somewhere beyond the blue

The angels beckon me

From heaven's open door

And I can't feel at home in this world anymore.

The hymn could be understood to be telling workers to accept hunger and pain and not fight back. This angered Guthrie, so he mocked and parodied the original— keeping the melody and reworking the words to comment on the harsh material conditions many suffered through. "I ain't got no home, I'm just a-ramblin' round," he sang, talking about being a homeless, wandering worker who gets hassled by the police, rather than a subservient, spiritual traveler waiting for an afterlife door prize. Instead of looking to heaven— because "I can't feel at home in this world anymore"— Guthrie wryly arrived at his song's punch line: "I ain't got no home in this world anymore."[3]

In 1940 Guthrie was bombarded by Irving Berlin's jingoistic "God Bless America," which goes, in part, "From the mountains to the prairies / to the oceans white with foam / God bless America, my home sweet home." The irritated folk singer wrote a response that originally went, "From California to the New York Island / From the Redwood forest to the Gulf Stream waters / God blessed America for me." (Guthrie later changed the last line to "This land was made for you and me.") Continuing with his anti-privatization theme, in another version of this famous song Guthrie wrote:

As I was walkin'— I saw a sign there

And that sign said— no trespassin'

But on the other side . . . it didn't say nothin'!

Now that side was made for you and me!

He set the lyrics to a beautiful melody he learned from the Carter Family, giving birth to one of the most enduring (and endearing) folk songs of all time. Guthrie's approach is a great example of how appropriation— stealing, borrowing, whatever you want to call it— is a creative act that can have a powerful impact. Before Guthrie, the Industrial Workers of the World, the Wobblies, borrowed from popular melodies for their radical tunes, which were published and popularized in the *Little Red Songbook*. These songs also parodied religious hymns, such as "In the Sweet By-and-By," which was changed to, "You will eat, by and by."[4]

For Guthrie and many other folk musicians, music *was* politics. Guthrie was affiliated closely with the labor movement, which inspired many of his greatest songs; these songs, in turn, motivated members of the movement during trying times. That's why Guthrie famously scrawled on his guitar, "This Machine Kills Fascists." Appropriation is an important method that creative people have used to comment on the world for years, from the radical Dada art of the early twentieth century to the beats and rhymes of hip-hop artists today. Guthrie drew from the culture that surrounded him and transformed, reworked, and remixed it in order to write moving songs that inspired the working class to fight for a dignified life. Instead of passively consuming and regurgitating the Tin Pan Alley songs that were popular during the day, Guthrie and other folk singers *created* culture in an attempt to change the world around them. They were truly part of a counterculture, not an over-the-counter culture.

Curious about the copyright status of Guthrie's decades-old music, I called up Woody Guthrie Publishing and spoke to a very nice gentleman named Michael Smith, the general manager of the organization. He was clearly familiar with the folk-song tradition and obviously knowledgeable about Guthrie, but he nevertheless had a lot of trouble accepting the idea that copyright extension was a bad thing for art and culture. I was surprised when Smith told me that the song-publishing company that owns Guthrie's music denies recording artists permission to adapt his lyrics. And I was shocked when Smith defended the actions of the company, called The Richmond Organization (TRO), even after I pointed out that Guthrie often altered other songwriters' lyrics. "Well," Smith explained, "he admitted to stealing, but at the time that Woody was writing . . ."He paused. "I mean, things have changed from Woody's time."

They certainly have. During the 2004 election season, a year after I spoke to Michael Smith, a small-time team of cartoonists posted a Guthrie-invoking political parody on their Web site. Not surprisingly, TRO threatened to sue. The animated short portrayed G.W. Bush and John Kerry singing a goofy ditty to the tune of "This Land Is Your Land," where Bush said, "You're a liberal sissy," Kerry replied, "You're a right wing nut job," and they sang together, "This land will surely vote for me." Guthrie's copyright managers didn't think it was funny at all. "This puts a completely different spin on the song," TRO's Kathryn Ostien told CNN. "The damage to the song is huge." Perhaps more damage is done to Guthrie's legacy by practicing such an aggressive form of copyright zealotry.

"If someone changed a lyric in Woody's time," said Michael Smith, "chances are it wasn't going to be recorded and it was just spread through campfire singing, you know, family-time singing and stuff like that. You know, now you can create your own CD at home and distribute it any way you want to, and so the dissemination is a lot broader, a lot faster, and can be a lot more detrimental to the integrity of the song."*Detrimental to the integrity of the song?* I pressed him further on Guthrie's own alterations of others' songs and asked what Woody would think of TRO locking up his folksong catalog. "The answer to that is, you know, 'Hey, you're going to have to ask him, because we have a duty,' " Smith said. "We don't know what Woody would have wanted— we can't tell."

Soon Michael Smith began to make a little more sense to me— at least economic sense. "If you allow multiple rewrites to occur, then people will think it's in the public domain, and then you have a hard time pressing people to prove to them that it's not in the public domain." Then the publishers can no longer generate revenue from it. That a company can still make money off "This Land Is Your Land" is exactly the type of thing I believe Woody Guthrie *would not* have wanted. Even worse, that TRO prevents musicians from releasing altered, updated versions of his music probably makes Guthrie roll in his grave. But don't trust me; listen to the man himself. When Guthrie was still alive, for instance, Bess Lomax Hawes told him that his song "Union Maid" had gone into the oral tradition, as folklorists call it.

"It was part of the cultural landscape, no longer even associated with him," said Hawes, the daughter of the famous song collector and archivist Alan Lomax."He answered, 'If that were true, it would be the greatest honor of my life.' "[5] In a written statement attached to a published copy of his lyrics for "This Land Is Your Land," Guthrie made clear his belief that it should be understood as communal property. "This song is Copyrighted in US," he wrote, "under Seal of Copyright # 154085, for a period of 28 years, and anybody caught singin' it without our permission will be mighty good friends of ours, cause we don't give a dern. Publish it. Write it. Sing it. Swing to it. Yodel it. We wrote it, that's all we wanted to do." Notice that he mentioned the song's copyright lasted twenty-eight years, though the term was later lengthened.

Also note that Guthrie said, "We wrote it" not *"I* wrote it," something that indicates Guthrie didn't see himself as the song's sole author. Since much of the song's power comes from that lovely melody passed down to him, how could he? In light of Guthrie's view, how sad it is that others continue to taint this socialist musician's ideals by keeping his songs private property, turning them into a lucrative revenue stream rather than a shareable part of our common cultural heritage. If Woody Guthrie had to make his art under the overly restrictive policies his song-publishing company imposes on today's musicians, it would have been very hard for him to make his music at all. In some cases it would have been impossible, for "things have changed."

In a dramatic turn of events, Ludlow Music, the subsidiary of TRO that controls Guthrie's most famous copyrights, backed off from its legal threats against JibJab.com's parody. This was after the Electronic Frontier Foundation (EFF)—a nonprofit organization that defends civil liberties online— came to the Web site's rescue, providing legal counsel. What made the aftermath of the JibJab.com flap remarkable wasn't merely that the copyright bullying ended. More interesting was the discovery by EFF senior intellectual property attorney Fred von Lohmann that, according to his research, "This Land Is Your Land" has been in the public domain since 1973! He writes:

Fact#1: Guthrie wrote the song in 1940. At that time, the term of copyright was twenty-eight years, renewable once for an additional twenty-eight years. Under the relevant law, the copyright term for a song begins when the song is published as sheet music. (Just performing it is not enough to trigger the clock.)

Fact #2: A search of Copyright Office records shows that the copyright wasn't registered until 1956, and Ludlow filed for a renewal in 1984.

Fact #3: Thanks to tips provided by musicologists who heard about this story, we discovered that Guthrie published and sold the sheet music for "This Land Is Your Land" in a pamphlet in 1945. An original copy of this mimeograph was located for us by generous volunteers who visited the Library of Congress in Washington, D.C. This means that the copyright in the song expired in 1973, twenty-eight years after Guthrie published the sheet music. Ludlow's attempted renewal in

1984 was eleven years tardy, which means the classic Guthrie song is in the public domain. (I'll note that Ludlow disputes this, although I've not heard any credible explanation from them.)

So Guthrie's original joins "The Star-Spangled Banner," "Amazing Grace," and Beethoven's Symphonies in the public domain. Come to think of it, now that "This Land Is Your Land" is in the public domain, can we make it our national anthem? That would be the most fitting ending of all.

Because art isn't made from thin air, the existence of a large and thriving public domain enriches the quality and diversity of creative expression. It's an important resource used by creative people to make new works, such as the musicals *Les Misérables* (based on the nineteenth-century novel by Victor Hugo) and *West Side Story* (based on Shakespeare's *Romeo and Juliet)*.[6] The public domain also promotes artistic freedom of expression®, because it eliminates the rigid control some copyright owners exercise over the context in which their works appear. For instance, Gilbert and Sullivan's comic operas were tightly controlled by the D'Oyly Carte Opera, which required that all performances be staged exactly as the originals were. Not a note could change. But when the copyrights were released into the public domain the musicals were freed from the shackles of artistic mummification.[7]

Disney— which strongly lobbied for the Bono Act— made billions of dollars recycling "Snow White," "Pinocchio," "Beauty and the Beast," and many other old stories and fables. Like Guthrie, it would have been much harder for Walt Disney to legally make his fortune if he had to work under the intellectual-property laws his corporate heirs advocate. In his dissenting opinion in the challenge to the Bono Act, which the Supreme Court upheld, Justice Stephen Breyer argued that this law threatens the endangered ecosystem that is our cultural commons. "I cannot find," wrote Breyer, "any constitutionally legitimate, copyrighted-related way in which the statute will benefit the public. Indeed, in respect to existing works, the serious public harm and the virtually nonexistent public benefit could not be more clear."

Copyright protectionists defend the Bono Act by pointing out that Congress was only adhering to international copyright standards. However, this assertion ignores the fact that U.S.–based corporations such as Disney had a hugely influential role in setting these standards. In 2003 Illegal Art— a label hosted by Steev Hise's collage-centric Web site detritus.net and run by the pseudonymously named Philo Farnsworth (after the inventor of the television)— fought back. The label began work on its latest project, a compilation CD named *Sonny Bono Is Dead.* In its press release soliciting the input of artists, Illegal Art stated, "We encourage artists to liberally sample from works that would have fallen into the Public Domain by the year 2004 had the Sonny Bono Act failed," adding slyly that "artists are also encouraged to create new works by sampling Sonny Bono's output."

[This essay originally appeared in the author's book, *Freedom of Expression®.*]

ABOUT THE AUTHORS
LISTED BY ORDER OF APPEARANCE

Marcus Kesler is the chairman of the Pirate Party of Oklahoma.

Ryan Moffitt is a free speech and civil liberties activist from Plano, Texas. He is the co-founder and current chairman of the Florida Pirate Party, and is presently heavily engaged in a campaign for a state senate seat from Palm Beach County, Florida. The Florida Pirate Party website can be found at http://fl.pirate.is.

Howard Denson worked for several newspapers before spending nearly four decades as a teacher of English and humanities at what is now Florida State College at Jacksonville. He has edited or written for such periodicals as *The State Street Review*, *Penchant* (for the Florida First Coast Writers' Festival), *The Write Stuff* (for the North Florida Writers), the *FCCJ Update*, and even*The International Journal of Elvisology and the Elvisian Era*. He blogs at http://howarddenson.webs.com/apps/blog/.

Reagen Dandridge Desilets resides with her husband and three children in the beautiful South Carolina Lowcountry. She first became interested in politics, beyond just voting, in 2008. She's gone from once being a straight-ticket GOP voter to a free-market libertarian and agorist. Those that have helped her better understand politics and economics include friend, activist, and author, Tarrin P. Lupo as well as Murray Rothbard and Friedrich Hayek.

In her agorist ventures, Reagen has found a niche in the world of publishing and has been working with self-published authors since July of 2010, starting with Tarrin (http://LupoLit.com). She has worked on all of his books, primarily with creative editing as well as print layout and ebook layout, and created and admins his websites. She is currently working with several more authors helping them convert from print to ebook and finding the right places to market them online, and is open to inquiries from anyone interested in publishing their own book. She believes wholeheartedly in the free market and is glad to be able to take part in helping the literary industry become more varied and diverse.

Reagen's other interests include volunteering and reenacting, urban exploration, photography, writing, art (sketching and painting watercolors), and learning to live naturally. She spends time painting and playing with her children and helping them to better understand the world around them, from nature to politics. She has several books of her own in progress and hopes to have at least one complete and available by the end of 2011.

Reagen can be contacted via Twitter @redd4a3 or email at redd4a3 at yahoo dot com.

Andrew "K'Tetch" Norton is a politicized engineer. British born, he now lives with his wife and three children in the state of Georgia, where he analyzes technology, and political practices. He was the first recognized head of Pirate Party International, a post he took on after almost a year and a half running the US party. He has been involved in politics for almost 15 years, including time spent with the Liberal Party and Conservative Party in the UK and the Libertarian Party in the US. His hobbies include science fiction, astronomy, and particle physics, and his core belief is that Personal Integrity and Honesty is the core to a functional society. He blogs at http://falkvinge.net and his own site, http://ktetch.blogspot.com/. He also Tweets @ktetch.

William Sims Bainbridge earned his doctorate in sociology from Harvard University, taught in universities for twenty years, and then joined the National Science Foundation, where he currently is a program director in Human-Centered Computing. He is author or co-author of 20 scientific books and over 200 shorter publications. Several of his major projects were based on computer software he programmed, most recently the 2006 book *God from the Machine: Artificial Intelligence Models of Religious Cognition*. Four of his earlier projects were textbook-software packages, and three books focused on the sociology of space exploration. He has also published extensively in the sociology of religion, notably *The Sociology of Religious Movements* (1997) and *Across the Secular Abyss* (2007). Most recently he has written about virtual gameworlds in *Online Multiplayer Games* (2010), *The Warcraft Civilization* (2010), and *The Virtual Future* (2011). He edited a pair of two-volume reference works, *Encyclopedia of Human-Computer Interaction* (2004) and *Leadership in Science and Technology* (2012), plus the proceedings of the first major scientific conference held inside a computer game, *Online Worlds* (2010).

A journalist, activist, artist, and professor in the Department of Communication Studies at the University of Iowa, **Kembrew McLeod** is the author of *Owning Culture: Authorship, Ownership, and Intellectual Property Law* and has written music criticism for *Rolling Stone, The Village Voice, Spin, Mojo,* and the 2004 edition of the *New Rolling Stone Album Guide*. He is also the co-producer of a documentary on intellectual-property law, *Copyright Criminals: This Is a Sampling Sport,* which is currently in production, and he worked as a documentary producer at the Media Education Foundation. McLeod was involved in the traveling art show *Illegal Art: Freedom of Expression in the Corporate Age,* which traveled to New York, Chicago,Washington,D.C., and was hosted by the San Francisco Museum of Modern Art's Artist Gallery in 2003. You can download some of his work from his Web site, http://kembrew.com.

Dr. danah boyd is a Senior Researcher at Microsoft Research, a Research Assistant Professor in Media, Culture, and Communication at New York University, a Visiting Researcher at Harvard Law School and an Adjunct Associate Professor at the University of New South Wales. Her work examines everyday practices involving social media, with specific attention to youth engagement, privacy, and risky behaviors. She recently co-authored *Hanging Out, Messing Around, and Geeking Out: Kids Living and Learning With New Media.* She co-directed the Youth and Media Policy Working Group,funded by the MacArthur Foundation. She blogs at http://www.zephoria.org/thoughts/and tweets at @zephoria.

Travis McCrea is a 21 year old activist and entrepreneur, formerly an officer of the United States Pirate Party. He has moved to Canada and has run for Parliament through Pirate Party Canada, and uses direct action to protect civil liberties and the internet. He blogs at http://falkvinge.net and his own site, http://travismccrea.com.

Loreley MacTavish is a staunch supporter of human rights and privacy. She is an intensely private individual. She only agreed to allow us to run her piece in this book on the condition that we not divulge her identity. It is sad that such a remarkable person feels compelled to hide behind a curtain such as this, but these are the times we live in.

The **United Nations** is an international organization founded in 1945 after the Second World War by 51 countries committed to maintaining international peace and security, developing friendly relations among nations and promoting social progress, better living standards and human rights. Their website is http://un.org.

Rick Falkvinge is the founder of the first Pirate Party and is a political evangelist, traveling around Europe and the world to talk and write about ideas of a sensible information policy. He is also a net activist, building tunnels and tools whenever and wherever. His website is http://falkvinge.net. He may also be found on Twitter at @Falkvinge.

United States Pirate Party

Cory Doctorow (http://craphound.com) is a science fiction author, activist, journalist, and blogger – the co-editor of Boing Boing (http://boingboing.net) and the author of Tor Teens/HarperCollins UK novels like FOR THE WIN and the bestselling LITTLE BROTHER. He is the former European director of the Electronic Frontier Foundation and co-founded the UK Open Rights Group. Born in Toronto, Canada, he now lives in London.

Lawrence Lessig is a professor at Harvard Law School and is a director of the Edmond J. Safra Foundation Center for Ethics. The author of *The Future of Ideas, Code: And Other Laws of Cyberspace, Free Culture, Remix*, and *Republic, Lost*, he is the chair of the Creative Commons project (http://creativecommons.org). He studied at the University of Pennsylvania, Cambridge University, and Yale Law School, and he clerked for Judge Richard Posner of the U.S. Seventh Circuit Court of Appeals. His website is http://lessig.org.

Brad Hall is the vice-chairman of the Florida Pirate Party and spokesman for the United States Pirate Party. He has been involved in Pirate Politics since 2009.

Nina Paley is the creator of the animated musical feature film *Sita Sings the Blues*, which has screened in over 150 film festivals and won over 35 international awards including the Annecy Grand Crystal, The IFFLA Grand Jury Prize, and a Gotham Award. Her adventures in our broken copyright system led her to copyLeft her film, and join QuestionCopyright.org as Artist-in-Residence. Prior to becoming an animator Nina was a syndicated cartoonist; she is now re-releasing all her old comics under a Creative Commons Share-Alike license. A 2006 Guggenheim Fellow, Nina is currently producing a series of animated shorts about intellectual freedom called Minute Memes.

http://www.ninapaley.com

http://www.sitasingstheblues.com/

http://questioncopyright.org/

http://mimiandeunice.com/

From the Internet to the iPod, technologies are transforming our society and empowering us as speakers, citizens, creators, and consumers. When our freedoms in the networked world come under attack, the **Electronic Frontier Foundation** (EFF) is the first line of defense. EFF broke new ground when it was founded in 1990 — well before the Internet was on most people's radar — and continues to confront cutting-edge issues defending free speech, privacy, innovation, and consumer rights today. From the beginning, EFF has championed the public interest in every critical battle affecting digital rights.

Blending the expertise of lawyers, policy analysts, activists, and technologists, EFF achieves significant victories on behalf of consumers and the general public. EFF fights for freedom primarily in the courts, bringing and defending lawsuits even when that means taking on the US government or large corporations. By mobilizing more than 61,000 concerned citizens through our Action Center, EFF beats back bad legislation. In addition to advising policymakers, EFF educates the press and public.

http://eff.org/

FURTHER READING

No one becomes an expert in a field by reading just one book, no matter how good it is. Below is a (non-exhaustive) list of books that we feel you would enjoy if you enjoyed this one. Also, some of the below listed books may be either freely available from the author's website, or be released under a Creative Commons license. Many of the CC licensed books may be found at the United States Pirate Party Library, found online at http://wiki.pirate.is/index.php?title=Library. We are always looking for more books to read.

These books cover a range of topics, some of which were not covered in this book.

Access Denied edited by Ronald Deibert, John Palfrey, Rafal Rohozinski, and Jonathan Zittrain

Against Intellectual Monopoly by Michele Boldrin and David K. Levine

Against Intellectual Property by N. Stephan Kinsella

Arts, Inc. by Bill Ivey

Code: And Other Laws of Cyberspace by Lawrence Lessig

Common As Air by Lewis Hyde

Content by Cory Doctorow

Context by Cory Doctorow

Digitize This Book by Gary Hall

Edited Clean Version by Raiford Guins

Failed States: The Abuse of Power and the Assault on Democracy by Noam Chomsky

Freakonomics by Steven D. Levitt & Stephen J. Dubner

Free by Chris Anderson

Free Culture by Lawrence Lessig

Freedom of Expression by Kembew McLeod

From Shakespeare to DJ Danger Mouse: A Quick Look at Copyright and User Creativity in the Digital Age by Urs Gasser and Silke Ernst

Gridlock Economy by Michael Heller

Jokapiraatinoikeus (Every Pirate's Right) (Finnish) by Ahto Apajalahti and Kaj Sotala

Little Brother by Cory Doctorow

Macrowikinomics by Don Tapscott and Anthony D. Williams

Mashed Up by Aram Sinnreich

Moral Panics and the Copyright Wars by William Patry

Nemesis: The Last Days of the American Republic (American Empire Project) by Chalmers Johnson

United States Pirate Party

No Law by David L. Lange and H. Jefferson Powell

Piracy by Adrian Johns

Privacy and Free Speech: It's Good for Business by the ACLU of North Carolina

Reality Hunger by David Shields

Rebooting America: Ideas for Redesigning American Democracy for the Internet Age by the Personal Democracy Press

Remix by Lawrence Lessig

Republic, Lost by Lawrence Lessig

*Super Freakonomic*s by Steven D. Levitt & Stephen J. Dubner

The Law of Cyberspace: An Invitation to the Table of Negotiations by Ahmad Kamal

*The Future of Idea*s by Lawrence Lessig

The Long Tail by Chris Anderson

The Pirate's Dilemma by Matt Mason

The Return of Depression Economics by Paul Krugman

The Shallows by Nicholas Carr

The World is Flat by Thomas L. Friedman

Wealth of Networks: How Social Production Transforms Markets and Freedom by Yochai Benkler

Wikinomics by Don Tapscott and Anthony D. Williams

What Technology Wants by Kevin Kelly

REFERENCES

References for Assassinating Citizens:

[1]Washington Post, Judge Dismisses Targeted-Killing Suit,December 8th,2010. Retrieved September 30th, 2011.
http://online.wsj.com/article/SB10001424052748703296604576005391675065166.html?mod=googlenews_wsj

[2]US Supreme Court Center, Ohio v. Reiner on petition for Writ of Certiorari to the Supreme Court of Ohio,532 U.S. 17 (2001). Retrieved September 30th, 2011
http://supreme.justia.com/us/532/17/case.html

[3]Washington Post, Secret U.S. memo sanctioned killing of Aulaki,September 30th, 2011. Retrieved September 30th,2011.
http://www.washingtonpost.com/world/national-security/aulaqi-killing-reignites-debate-on-limits-of-executive-power/2011/09/30/gIQAx1bUAL_story.html

References for Parable of the Pasture

[1] Albionmonitor.net, Background on BIA Suit.
http://www.albionmonitor.com/0209a/0209a-404.html

United States Pirate Party
References for Fluid Democracy

Bainbridge, William Sims. 1986. *Dimensions of Science Fiction.* Cambridge: Harvard University Press.

Bainbridge, William Sims. 1991. *Goals in Space: American Values and the Future of Technology.* Albany, New York: State University of New York Press.

Bainbridge, William Sims. 1992. *Social Research Methods and Statistics: A Computer-Assisted Introduction.* Belmont, California: Wadsworth.

Bainbridge, William Sims. 1994. "Values." Pp. 4888-4892 in *The Encyclopedia of Language and Linguistics,* edited by R. E. Asher and J. M. Y. Simpson. Oxford: Pergamon.

Bainbridge, William Sims. 2000. "New Technologies for the Social Sciences." Pp. 111-126 in *Social Sciences for a Digital World,* edited by Marc Renaud. Paris: Organisation for Economic Co-Operation and Development.

Bainbridge, William Sims. 2003. "Privacy and Property on the Net: Research Questions." *Science* 302: 1686-1687.

Bainbridge, William Sims. 2004. "The Future of the Internet: Cultural and Individual Conceptions." Pp. 307-324 in *Society Online: The Internet in Context,* edited by P. N. Howard and S. Jones. Thousand Oaks, California: Sage.

Bainbridge, William Sims. 2007. "Expanding the Use of the Internet in Religious Research." *Review of Religious Research* 49(1): 7-20.

Bainbridge, William Sims. 2009a. "Motivations for Space Exploration." Futures 41:514-522.

Bainbridge, William Sims. 2009b. "Space: The Final Frontier." Futures 41: 511-513.

Bainbridge, William Sims (editor). 2010a. Online Worlds: Convergence of the Real and the Virtual. London: Springer.

Bainbridge, William Sims. 2010b. *The Warcraft Civilization*. Cambridge, Massachusetts: MIT Press.

Bainbridge, William Sims. 2011. "Peer Review." Pp. 389-396 in *Leadership in Science and Technology*, edited by W. S. Bainbridge. Thousand Oaks, California: Sage.

Basu, Chumki, Haym Hirsh, and William Cohen. 1998. "Recommendation as Classification: Using Social and Content-Based Information in Recommendation." *Proceedings of the Fifteenth National Conference on Artificial Intelligence*. Madison, Wisconsin.

Bohannon, John. 2008. "Scientists Invade Azeroth." *Science* 320:1592.

Bohannon, John. 2011. "Meeting for Peer Review at a Resort that's Virtually Free." *Science* 331: 27.

Börner, Katy. 2010. Atlas of Science: Visualizing What We Know. Cambridge, Massachusetts: MIT Press.

Börner, Katy. 2011. "Network Science: Theory, Tools, and Practice." Pp 49-59 in *Leadership in Science and Technology*, edited by W. S. Bainbridge. Thousand Oaks, California: Sage.

Canny, John. 2002. "Collaborative Filtering with Privacy via Factor Analysis." Pp. 238-245 in *Proceedings of the 25th Annual International ACM SIGIR Conference on Research and Development in Information Retrieval*. New York: ACM.

Durkheim, Emile. 1897. *Suicide*. New York: Free Press [1951].

Ganz-Brown, Carole A. 1998. "Electronic Information Markets: An Idea Whose Time Has Come." *The Journal of World Intellectual Property* 1: 465–493.

Herlocker, Jonathan L., Joseph A. Konstan, Loren G. Terveen, and John T. Riedl. 2004. "Evaluating Collaborative Filtering Recommender Systems." *ACM Transactions on Information Systems* 22:5-53.

Howard, Philip N. 2011. *The Digital Origins of Dictatorship and Democracy: Information Technology and Political Islam.* New York: Oxford University Press.

Levi-Strauss, Claude. 1969. *The Elementary Structures of Kinship.* Boston, Beacon Press.

Malinowski, Bronislaw. 1927. *Sex and Repression in Savage Society.* New York: Harcourt, Brace.

Merton, Robert K. 1938. "Social Structure and Anomie." Pp. 185-214 in *Social Theory and Social Structure.* New York: Free Press [1968].

National Research Council. 2000. *The Digital Dilemma: Intellectual Property in the Information Age.* Washington, DC, 2000: National Academy Press.

Page, Lawrence, Sergey Brin, Rajeev Motwani, and Terry Winograd. 1998. "The PageRank Citation Ranking: Bringing Order to the Web." Technical Report, Stanford InfoLab.

Parsons, Talcott, and Edward A. Shils (eds.). 1951. *Toward a General Theory of Action.* Cambridge, Massachusetts: Harvard University Press.

Smelser, Neil J. 1962. *Theory of Collective Behavior.* New York: Free Press.

Tonn, Bruce, and Feldman, David. 1995. "Non-Spatial Government." *Futures* 27: 11-36.

Witte, James C., Lisa M. Amoroso, and Philip E. N. Howard. 2000. "Method and Representation in Internet-based Survey Tools: Mobility,

Community, and Cultural Identity in Survey2000." *Social Science Computer Review* 18: 179-195.

Web Pages

URL 1: http://wiki.piratenpartei.de/Liquid_Democracy; accessed and translated, October 21, 2011.

URL 2: http://ilpubs.stanford.edu:8090/422/1/1999-66.pdf

URL 3: http://en.wikipedia.org/wiki/Netflix_Prize

URL 4: http://www.blackhawksguild.com/index.php?name=FAQ&cat=1#11

URL 5: http://sda.berkeley.edu/archive.htm

URL 6: http://mysite.verizon.net/wsbainbridge/system/goals.pdf

URL 7: http://mysite.verizon.net/wsbainbridge/system/software.htm

URL 8: http://www.tva.com/abouttva/history.htm

References for Privatizing Life

[1] *Washington Post,* To own the human genome, 1998; P. Cohen, *New Scientist;* T.Wilkie, *Independent* (London), 1995.

[2] J. Gillis,*Washington Post,* 1999.

[3] D. Bollier, *Silent Theft.*

[4] F. Bowring, *Science, seeds and cyborgs.*

[5] D. Charles, *Lords of the harvest,* p. 185.

[6] F. Bowring, *Science, seeds and cyborgs.*

[7] P. Pringle, *Food, Inc.;* A. Duffy, *Ottawa Citizen,* 1998.

[8] *NOW with Bill Moyers,* Seeds of conflict.

[9] T.McGirk, *Time* (international edition, Asia); V. Shiva, *Biopiracy;* N. Roht-Arriaza, *Borrowed power,* p. 259.

[10] V. Shiva, *Protect or plunder?*

[11] Ibid.

[12] P. Pringle, *Food, Inc.;* K. Dawkins, *Gene wars.*

[13] K. Dawkins, *Gene wars;* P. Pringle, *Food, Inc.;* S. Shulman, *Owning the future,* p. 110; K. E. Maskus, *Intellectual property rights in the global economy.*

[14] E. H.Wirtén, *No trespassing.*

[15] P. Drahos with J. Braithwaite, *Information feudalism,* p. 10.

[16] K. E. Maskus, *Intellectual property rights in the global economy;* V. Shiva, *Protect or plunder?*; P. Drahos with J. Braithwaite, *Information feudalism.*

[17] F. Bowring, *Science, seeds and cyborgs.*

[18] S.Meyer, *Paradoxes of fame.*

References for Killing The Corporate Person

[1] 1 U.S.C. §1

[2] Citizens United v. Federal Election Commission, 558 U.S. 08-205 (2010)

[3] "Fatalities Associated With Crash Induced Fuel Leakage and Fires," by E.S. Grush and C.S. Saundy, Environmental and Safety Engineering (1973)

References for No Safe Quarter

[1] http://www.youtube.com/watch?v=A6e7wfDHzew

[2] http://rt.com/usa/news/harwood-intellistreets-hills-farmington-321/

References for History of Copyright

https://secure.wikimedia.org/wikipedia/en/wiki/Censorship_in_France#To_the_18th_century

http://questioncopyright.org/promise

http://www.flowofhistory.com/units/west/11/FC74

https://secure.wikimedia.org/wikipedia/en/wiki/Mary_I_of_England

https://secure.wikimedia.org/wikipedia/en/wiki/Worshipful_Company_of_Stationers_and_Newspaper_Makers

http://copyriot.se/2008/04/08/what-the-ifpi-tries-to-conceal-about-its-origins-in-fascist-italy/

http://translate.google.com/translate?js=n&prev=_t&hl=en&ie=UTF-8&layout=2&eotf=1&sl=auto&tl=en&u=http://www.expressen.se/kultur/1.1384757/upphovsrota

http://www.amazon.com/Information-Feudalism-Owns-Knowledge-

Economy/dp/1595581227/ref=tmm_pap_title_0/176-5202348-4305869

http://en.wikipedia.org/wiki/Habeas_Corpus_Act_1640

http://en.wikipedia.org/wiki/Star_Chamber

http://en.wikipedia.org/wiki/Licensing_Order_of_1643

http://en.wikipedia.org/wiki/Entick_v_Carrington

http://en.wikipedia.org/wiki/Copyright_Clause

http://www.pddoc.com/copyright/promote_progess.htm

http://www.movingtofreedom.org/2006/10/06/thomas-jefferson-on-patents-and-freedom-of-ideas/

http://www.spiegel.de/international/zeitgeist/0,1518,710976,00.html

http://falkvinge.net/2011/01/21/there-are-three-parties-to-copyright/

http://falkvinge.net/2011/02/08/history-of-copyright-part-4-the-us-and-libraries/

http://www.wipo.int/treaties/en/ip/berne/trtdocs_wo001.html

http://en.wikipedia.org/wiki/International_Labour_Organization

http://en.wikipedia.org/wiki/Estado_Novo_(Portugal)

http://torrentfreak.com/do-you-prefer-copyright-or-the-right-to-talk-in-private-110121/

http://en.wikipedia.org/wiki/GATT

http://en.wikipedia.org/wiki/AllOfMp3

http://falkvinge.net/2011/02/07/copyright-as-a-fundamentalist-religion/

[1] I am grateful to Peter DiMauro for pointing me to this extraordinary history. See also Siva Vaidhyanathan, *Copyrights and Copywrongs,* 87–93, which details Edison's "adventures" with copyright and patent.

[2] J. A. Aberdeen, *Hollywood Renegades: The Society of Independent Motion]Picture Producers* (Cobblestone Entertainment, 2000) and expanded texts posted at "The Edison Movie Monopoly: The Motion Picture Patents Company vs. the Independent Outlaws," available at link the link listed below. For a discussion of the economic motive behind both these limits and the limits imposed by Victor on phonographs, see Randal C. Picker, "From Edison to the Broadcast Flag: Mechanisms of Consent and Refusal and the Propertization of Copyright" (September 2002), University of Chicago Law School, James M. Olin Program in Law and Economics, Working Paper No. 159.

http://www.cobbles.com/simpp_archive/edison_trust.htm

[3] Marc Wanamaker, "The First Studios," *The Silents Majority,* archived at http://free-culture.cc/notes/12.pdf.

[4] To Amend and Consolidate the Acts Respecting Copyright: Hearings on S. 6330 and H.R. 19853 Before the (Joint) Committees on Patents, 59th Cong. 59, 1st sess. (1906) (statement of Senator Alfred B. Kittredge, of South Dakota, chairman), reprinted in *Legislative History of the 1909 Copyright Act,* E. Fulton Brylawski and Abe Goldman, eds. (South Hackensack, N.J.: Rothman Reprints, 1976).

[5] To Amend and Consolidate the Acts Respecting Copyright, 223 (statement of Nathan Burkan, attorney for the Music Publishers Association).

[6]. To Amend and Consolidate the Acts Respecting Copyright, 226 (statementof Nathan Burkan, attorney for the Music Publishers Association).

[7] To Amend and Consolidate the Acts Respecting Copyright, 23 (statement of John Philip Sousa, composer).

[8] To Amend and Consolidate the Acts Respecting Copyright, 283–84 (statement of Albert Walker, representative of the Auto-Music Perforating Company of New York).

[9] To Amend and Consolidate the Acts Respecting Copyright, 376 (prepared memorandum of Philip Mauro, general patent counsel of the American Graphophone Company Association).

[10] Copyright Law Revision: Hearings on S. 2499, S. 2900, H.R. 243, and H.R. 11794 Before the (Joint) Committee on Patents, 60th Cong., 1st sess., 217 (1908) (statement of Senator Reed Smoot, chairman), reprinted in *Legislative History of the 1909 Copyright Act,* E. Fulton Brylawski and Abe Goldman, eds. (South Hackensack, N.J.: Rothman Reprints, 1976).

[11] Copyright Law Revision: Report to Accompany H.R. 2512, House Committee on the Judiciary, 90th Cong., 1st sess., House Document no. 83, 66 (8 March 1967). I am grateful to Glenn Brown for drawing my attention to this report.

[12] See 17 *United States Code,* sections 106 and 110. At the beginning, record companies printed "Not Licensed for Radio Broadcast" and other messages purporting to restrict the ability to play a record on a radio station. Judge Learned Hand rejected the argument that a warning attached to a record might restrict the rights of the radio station. See *RCA Manufacturing Co.* v. *Whiteman,* 114 F. 2d 86 (2nd Cir. 1940). See also Randal C. Picker, "From Edison to the Broadcast Flag: Mechanisms of Consent and Refusal and the Propertization of Copyright," *University of Chicago Law Review* 70 (2003): 281.

[13] Copyright Law Revision—CATV: Hearing on S. 1006 Before the Subcommittee on Patents, Trademarks, and Copyrights of the Senate Committee on the Judiciary, 89th Cong., 2nd sess., 78 (1966) (statement of Rosel H. Hyde, chairman of the Federal Communications Commission).

[14]. Copyright Law Revision—CATV, 116 (statement of Douglas A. Anello, general counsel of the National Association of Broadcasters).

[15] Copyright Law Revision—CATV, 126 (statement of Ernest W. Jennes, general counsel of the Association of Maximum Service Telecasters, Inc.).

[16] Copyright Law Revision—CATV, 169 (joint statement of Arthur B.Krim, president of United Artists Corp., and John Sinn, president of United Artists Television, Inc.).

[17] Copyright Law Revision—CATV, 209 (statement of Charlton Heston, president of the Screen Actors Guild).

[18] Copyright Law Revision—CATV, 216 (statement of Edwin M. Zimmerman, acting assistant attorney general).

[19] See, for example,National Music Publisher's Association, *The Engine of Free Expression: Copyright on the Internet—The Myth of Free Information,* available at http://www.nmpa.org/music101/copyrights.asp. "The threat of piracy —the use of someone else's creative work without permission or compensation—has grown with the Internet."

Questions About Copyright

[1] http://intellectualeconomy.wordpress.com/2010/06/08/coalition-of-manga-publishers/

[2] http://en.wikipedia.org/wiki/Audio_Home_Recording_Act

[3] http://intellectualeconomy.wordpress.com/2011/12/29/a-story-from-a-few-days-ago/

[4] http://copyright.cornell.edu/resources/publicdomain.cfm

[5] http://www.crimeandpunishment.net/FL/chart.html

References for This Gene is Your Gene

[1] J. Shreeve, *The genome war,* p. 363.

[2] The offenders: Hank Thompson's "Wild Side of Life"; the Carter Family's "I'm Thinking Tonight of My Blue Eyes"; Roy Acuff's "Great Speckled Bird"; Kitty Wells's "It Wasn't God Who Made Honky Tonk Angels"; Reno and Smiley's "I'm Using My Bible as a

Roadmap"; and Townes Van Zant's "Heavenly Houseboat Blues."(I've since discovered many more.)

[3] J. Klein,*Woody Guthrie,* p. 120.

[4] Ibid., p. 82.

[5] S. Zeitlin, *New York Times,* 1998, p. A15.

[6] S. Fishman, *The public domain.*

[7] Ibid.

United States Pirate Party
GET INVOLVED!

The United States Pirate Party always needs more help. We are officially registered in two states (Massachusetts and Florida) and are working to be officially registered in every other state. Several states have a Pirate Party presense and need help to be set up by residents of those states. The other states need help and assistance as well.

Websites to reach the USPP:

http://us.pirate.is

http://pirate-party.us

Currently we hold meetings Tuesday evenings at 6:00 PM PST / 9:00 PM EST at http://wa.pirate.is/getinvolved/chat If you have your own IRC client you can use the following server irc.pirateirc.net port 6667 (or 6697 for SSL) and channel #uspp.

All are welcome to all meetings.

We can also be found on Facebook at
https://www.facebook.com/USPirateParty

We may also be found on Twitter under the name @USPirates

We are also looking for submissions for future editions of *No Safe Harbor*. For more information, contact brad.hall@pirate-party.us

www.ingramcontent.com/pod-product-compliance
Lightning Source LLC
Chambersburg PA
CBHW060243290526
45789CB00001B/167